THE SECOND CIVIL WAR

ARMING FOR ARMAGEDDON

OTHER BOOKS BY GARRY WILLS

Chesterton
Politics and Catholic Freedom
Roman Culture
Jack Ruby (with Ovid Demaris)

THE SECOND CIVIL WAR
ARMING FOR ARMAGEDDON

BY GARRY WILLS

 THE NEW AMERICAN LIBRARY

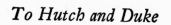

To Hutch and Duke

We do not, in this country now, have much taste for, or any real sense of, the extremes human beings can reach; time will improve us in this regard . . .

—JAMES BALDWIN

CONTENTS

THE SECOND CIVIL WAR

ARMING FOR ARMAGEDDON

PROLOGUE

There are few things in the world as
dangerous as sleepwalkers . . .

—RALPH ELLISON

In one of America's largest cities, the police officer in charge of Community Relations told me: "I have to work more on our men's attitudes than on the Negro community's. Police are constantly exposed to the seamiest side of life in the ghetto. Besides, a cop *has* to be suspicious if he is any good. And our men are scared. They take their lives in their hands every day they go to work. The last three policemen to be killed here were surprised before they could get at their weapons—and in each case, it was by a Negro assailant. Well, you know that's going to make the others pretty fast in getting their guns out. I hate to see the young kids become so callous so fast in their dealings with the Negroes. Young idealists enlist with us and become young cynics overnight. My department is supposed to prevent that, but I honestly don't know what to do about it."

His remarks had special force for me. I had been traveling from police department to police department across the country—nine major cities in two months—and spending most of my time with these cynical men; riding with them, whenever I could, into ghetto areas, where the constant rub against hostility, a steady prickle of danger, forms spiritual calluses. Cruising in police cars, I might (I was afraid) have been absorbing the policeman's attitudes—this attitude, at least: a resignation to armed conflict in our cities as something inevitable. Was I getting their thick skin, seeing danger around every corner, without their excuse? If so, I had to disregard things I thought I had been learning, reluctantly, by the repetition of the same themes in city after city.

I had begun the trip on a limited assignment: *Esquire's* editor wanted a report on the preparations being made for future riots. "Give us ten thousand words on it." Is it true, for instance, that Los Angeles County has a tank? That New York City has a plan for occupation of the city by U.S. troops? If so, isn't this a sign of panic? Ten thousand words should give me plenty of room to tsk-tsk at the disparities—kids in the street versus cops manning tanks. What is this, anyway—Hungary?

It seemed a rhetorical question when I began my odyssey —an odyssey in reverse; one that made me lose, in some measure, my home, the things I had taken for granted, had thought of as familiar and safe—as, oddest of all, *mine*. It had its comic side, though I was in no mood for laughing as I went from one command post to another in what seemed a large army's combat system. I suppose everyone, sooner or later, gets the feeling that, whatever his earlier experience of the country, he is finally "discovering America." But this was a discovery that seemed more like lobotomy: as I found out more things about my country, I knew it less. I was discovering an alien, armed place, not at all the one I had thought I was living in; one I knew continually less about, and admired less. My great "discovery" seemed all a process of erasure.

There was a suspicion, at the magazine, that the essay might not be all tanks and tsk-tsks. The editor had been impressed by something Norman Mailer told *Esquire's* staff at a luncheon held in his honor: "I have advocated more violence in American life, and now I have to live with that. But when men shoot at the firemen who are trying to put out the fire in their own homes, isn't that a civilization's way of committing suicide?"

That was the question that was surfacing, at last, in the wake of 1967's riots. Just before I began work on the article, Daniel P. Moynihan told the annual meeting of Americans for Democratic Action that "we must prepare for the onset of terrorism." If that were true, then perhaps the tanks were *needed*. The possibility had to be considered, anyway, before my tsk-tsking began.

But the question shifted its outlines as I asked it in Washington, Philadelphia, Chicago. The problem became less "Is this tank necessary?" and more "Do men *think* it necessary?" The answer to that was being given unambiguously by businessmen. In 1966, no armored personnel carriers were on display at the annual convention of the International Association of Chiefs of Police; no one dreamed they ever would be. But at the Kansas City meeting, in the fall of 1967, four cars were exhibited, and four more were advertised as in the planning stage. One officer of the IACP told me: "I thought, when I first entered the hall, I had come to a meeting of the Afrika Korps. Those were not police vehicles." The head of Michigan State University's School of Police Administration told me he thought most police would be laughed out of their communities if they asked for the money (up to $50,000) to buy one of those cars. He was wrong. Riot weapons of all sorts—including automatic rifles—have become a great new field for commercial competition. The police are buying everything politicians will let them; politicians are letting them buy everything the voters will allow; the voters are allowing (or demanding) more every day. And expensive things, once made, once bought, have a way of getting used.

The tanks are necessary if men feel they are—necessary

to *them,* obviously; useful, if only to quiet this longing for them, useful, in that sense, even if never used. The question realigns itself once more. Obviously men want the tanks. *Why* do they want them? Panic? Sheer sadism? But sadism and fear do not need such expensive adjuncts. Acute sadism is better practiced on the defenseless than on those who will do battle in the streets. Acute personal fear would drive men into less risky jobs than the deployment of tanks in street combat. As I talked to policemen across the country, I realized they do not feel an irresistible urge to beat Negroes or run from Negroes. They would simply prefer not to deal with them; and *if* they must deal with them, they want to do it as one manipulates some foreign substance, with gloves on, the thicker the better, gloves of steel. The tanks embody that psychic wall of separation the cop wants to pull around him when he moves into any group of Negroes. That is why they are necessary. My discovery had, then, the slightly ridiculous air that always surrounds a first realization of the obvious. We are two nations, white and black, strong and weak; and the stronger side wants to keep things that way, without "dirtying their hands" in the process. Furthermore, the white man's need to make it clear his is still the stronger side indicates a *shift* in the power-ratio, as well as an attempt to maintain it.

The police are not callous in the sense that they grow indifferent to humanity, hardened into monsters of dispassion or twisted passions. Like most people with emotionally wearing jobs, they adopt a clinical air at their work, deliberately one-dimensional. They suspend their normal emotions while on duty, saving up their tenderness for the children at home. Doctors and nurses do the same: total emotional involvement with the patients would be unhealthy. The very dress of the hospital—white, uniform, undifferentiated, sterile of interest—proclaims this impersonality to others (and, more important, to themselves).

The girl who faints at the sight of a dog run over in the street can watch surgical horrors with composure, once she is starched into her nurse's apron, bathed in the brightness of the operating room. In such a light, all details are equally accentuated, which mercifully lessens *drama*, the compelling eruption of *one* important thing.

The policeman, too, has to deal in "cases" or go insane. That is true of his dealings with the white criminal as well as the black. The difference lies in the fact that a "case" can become a fleshed human being again if the doctor meets him outside the hospital. So can the white criminal, for a cop. But not the Negro; or only a rare one, with the rare cop. It is difficult for a policeman to maintain that psychic tension involved in remembering his "case" is also a person—difficult enough, even with a white case. Next to impossible with black cases. In this, policemen do not differ from others. The Negro lies at the periphery of white sympathy; he is the first to be sacrificed if some emotional chill touches that perimeter and makes it shrink, convulsively, in contractions of self-preservation. We are two nations, and one saves "one's own" in a crisis, before rescuing members of a different tribe. The Negro is, in this sense, "other," not fully "us"; and if a white man thinks of "*my* country" in some moment of division, the Negro is clearly not part of that country to the extent that it *is* "mine."

What I was observing was the whole white attitude spelled out, out on the borders of sympathy, in the actions of police. The Negroes were right in personifying "whitey" as a cop. The policeman may not be the best representative of white attitudes taken in the gross, but he represents the shrinking of the white man into tribalism at moments of crisis—the daily crisis cops ride through, rare crises that touch other parts of the white community. He represents the white man in a time of tense confrontation, which is where growing numbers of black men are determined to meet him. They do well to come prepared for hostility.

What I could see "writ large" in cops I began to recognize, appropriately scaled down, everywhere else in this white country. Much of my time during those two months was spent in the air, which is not a bad place for discovering America. Strip it of its wings, sink the long tube straight down a shaft, and the jet plane would tell future ages more about our culture than most of the carefully stocked time capsules. On one flight, I sat rotating the little ball that hoses cool air over one's right knee during the wait before takeoff (when the air conditioner is not working). A stewardess was distributing last month's magazines, each in its floppy leather briefcase; she cooed at all the children she saw wrestling with their seatbelts—one part of her cheerfulness that seemed unforced. For adults, her smile was as uniform and packaged as the gum in her tray —white teeth all in a row like the Chiclets. Packaged Lolita, one with the "beauty queen," bunny, drum majorette, Rockette—all our safe half-erotic harems. The stewardess moves innocently to the drill of commerce, weaving her Rockette dance across America, never missing a step— until she comes to a Negro child.

The little girl was in the seat in front of me, trying to squirm out of her father's protective encirclement. The stewardess had no coos for her—only the barest number of Chiclets showing, dimly lipstick-smeared, between her woodenly smiling lips, as she offered the distrustful hedging father a magazine. ("Can he *read*, after all?" she said by her half-hearted way of shuffling the briefcases.) Most of those magazines had articles in them about something called the Negro revolt—articles that ask the question, "What do they want?" Her stiffening suggested she thought this man wanted *her*. So?—isn't that the point of this harem-game, that men should *want* their dancing attendants? But she will not play the game with one of "them," with the alien. Negroes have a way of making the games of modern life break down and reveal their silliness. They are felt to be intruders, death's-heads at the feast. There was a bomb planted in that jet. He was in the seat ahead of mine. And that made the jet a perfect representation of our culture.

In the stewardess's defense, it should be admitted that this passenger *dressed* the part of a death's-head—sandaled, Levi'd, irregularly patched about with beard and "natural." From principle, one had to assume, not poverty. He carried an expensive movie camera, and was traveling first class. For his part, he seemed to think the stewardess wanted his *daughter*, over whom he was hunched in cavernous protection. The girl was interested in the heavy sheathed magazines, but her father warned temptation off with an energetic shake of his "Afro." He knew he was intruding, and he wanted no pretense about it. Later, he tried inconspicuously to crane around his neighbor in the window seat, plying his camera: we were over the gashed Utah landscape, and lights dazzled off our wing-blade made it all unreal with irises. The man by the window offered to move. The Negro took this offer with suspicion. It is not his country he was photographing; and he was used to having this rubbed in. The Negro has traveled for years by his own "underground" itinerary, with the few points marked where he might stop and take his daughter to the bathroom. Swept over the Rockies in a rush, with an accompanying bathroom, he will not believe things have changed, down there—not in the tick-tack-toe little towns he sights, now, with his camera, toy places in the Sierras; not under the California palm trees toward which the plane lowers. Watts has streets lined with palm trees. Big deal—he had permission to look at the country through an expensive lense. Unlike whites, however, he *saw* it, with all its faults.

Not, primarily, faults of malice; we are as innocent as

stewardesses, most of us. Our crime is not that America is white, but that we do not even know it is. The Negro does. He knows it every time a policeman passes. That is when *power* speaks to him; and determination to keep that power white was clearly marked when, synchronized with the growth of Negro population in the cities, residence requirements were loosened for police recruits. Not only are there far more whites than blacks on, say, the Baltimore police force; there are more white cops from outside the city limits than black cops from inside. It is not a *city* police force so much as a *white* one. Suburbs supply mercenaries to the inner city. The white army of occupation is maintained. That is what the country wants; but it does not want to know that it wants it. The white man does not think of this country as white; but he is careful to keep it that way.

Tsk-tsking the police, then, seemed too easy, as I went on; and useless. It was becoming a matter of tsk-tsking myself for not seeing earlier that the *two* nations exist—a matter of moving about so much and so fast that I caught, as it were, a glimpse of myself from behind; and saw, for the first time, that I am white, that "we" are white, that "our" country is.

Progress, of a sort; but not of the comforting sort. The fact was borne in on me that this is two countries; but this only reinforced a likelihood that war could arise between the two. One reason whites are belatedly awakening to facts about *their* nation is that scattered black individuals across the land are proclaiming, against obvious geographic difficulties, that their separated brothers form a single nation. And many of those who have been awakened to the concept of two countries are determined that *their* side must win in any conflict between the two.

Only once before did we recognize that we were two countries, and that time the stronger part defeated the weaker, without creating unity. The underlying cause of the division between North and South has itself become the basis of our new division. Abolitionists rallying on the New Haven green sent off "Beecher's Bibles," firearms through whose barrels they preached to the South. In the summer of 1967, Negro rioters replied, through gun barrels, that the preacher had not learned his own lesson. The nation was not "reconstructed" as a single thing; the two things were reshuffled, along different lines—instead of North and South, white and black. As James Baldwin put it: "In exactly the same way that the South imagines that it 'knows' the Negro, the North imagines that it has set him free. Both camps are deluded."

The imbalance of power is even greater now than it was between the Union and the Confederacy—and the temptations of preponderant power cannot be underestimated. But another victory would be as inconclusive as the first one. Short of annihilating the weaker side entirely, how could a war lead to unity? The survivors would be more bitter than the Southerners, more scattered, attended by more sympathy from abroad. We would be where we are, except that division would be driven deeper; any further clash—short of broadening the conflict on racial lines across the world—would lead to the extermination of one side, not its absorption into a "union."

There is everything to be said against war, then. But that has never stopped men from fighting wars. Black leaders recognize openly the risk of genocide, yet go on in the determination to make "whitey" recognize their existence and dignity. The white community, meanwhile, does not think in terms like "genocide," but is acquiring arsenals that are capable of it. I went out believing in one country, which was not likely to commit suicide. I continued, however, forced to test new hypotheses—that a white country already exists; that a black community is rapidly coming into existence; and that the two are on a collision course. More and more I asked what had come to be the real questions—what *kind* of collision? how big? how inevitable? This book is an attempt to put down the answers I was given, by men who will, in some measure, decide the matter. It is fitting, I suppose, that some of the most incisive comments, recorded in my last chapter, came from two young men who are caught at dead center of the problem, men who are black, militant, yet politicians, and—improbably—law officers. They have survived, in their own persons, the conflict that is involving us all—which suggests that the country may survive and become one at last. In that hope, I dedicate my book to those two men.

I BATTLE PLANS

*The world was enormous and I could
go anywhere in it I chose—including
America: and I decided to return
here because I was afraid to.*

—JAMES BALDWIN

I began work on the riot-control article near my home in Baltimore, because trouble—which did not come —was expected there. It was a peaceful start, in an almost idyllic setting. Yet the air was full of strange things, all the more impressive because they did not need the ordnance-rhetoric of Newark or Detroit to make themselves felt.

Cars driving from Baltimore to Maryland's Eastern Shore are spiderwebbed across a span of Bay Bridge on single lanes bad for military transit; but as soon as a car turns down this wavy spaniel-ear of peninsula, it runs free on divided highway (double lanes both ways), which makes for rapid troop-movement. The trucks of the National Guard have made this run several times, on their way to Cambridge, as I was now. Today the wide lanes are somnolent; no weekend crowds on their way to Ocean City, no armies moving. Two hundred and fifty state police have poured into Cambridge, but that was during the night. The wide concrete parallels pass hypnotizingly, like bloated traintracks in a dream. I pass a military staging area, the police barracks at Easton, only a few cars in its parking lot—despite appearances, a secret headquarters, even now, for General George M. Gelston, who is in hiding there as I drive by in late September, 1967.

One passes through clammy zones of fish-smell as the Bay advances or retreats beside Route 50. This is an enclave of an older world preserved, like some human game-shelter, along the Atlantic seaboard—too *far* East to be "Eastern." Men here never had a chance to fight the Civil War, a deprivation they are earnestly trying to repair. I first met the Eastern Shore in that crusty old fellow who allowed a party of my friends, grudgingly, on his fishing boat, as if taking our money were doing us a favor. He spent the day enforcing, by his movements, some balletic scheme of segregation from the "foreigners" on his little nautical rocking horse. His only real communication with us came when he wheezed out the secret that his wife had been fooled for years into believing his hernia operation made him impotent. He told the story with explosive little spasms meant to suggest the range of gallantries this made possible, grasshopper feats of withered *amour*. But we suspected it was just a foxy way of introducing segregation into his bedroom, the ultimate apartness of this pristine American type.

I met my second specimen of pure Eastern Shore when I crossed the Choptank River, which forms the fishing inlet of Cambridge. "Skipjacks," those beautiful trim anachronisms that still fish commercially under sail, stank and peeled aristocratically in the harbor, oystery remnants of the past, like the captain of our fishing party, refusing to die. I had to find a Negro church where the BAF (Black Action Federation) was going to hold its meeting; I pulled into a gas station, asked my way from a man who was servicing an elderly Negro couple's car. When he heard

the name of the church, he jerked his face at me, a tangle
of angry capillaries: "What do you want to know for?"

"I want to attend a meeting."

"Get the *hell* out of this town." I had hit some psychic
brake, and his stop-light eyes were burning red. They
call them rednecks, but most of the bigots I have met were
red-*eyed*—not from booze so much as hate, which has its
own nimbus.

I stammered back that he could not kick me out of a
public facility—that fight, at least, had been fought and
won farther South. He had heard something about this,
wafted here from "overseas" (Washington), but "I'd be
glad to pay any fine for the pleasure of busting your ass."
The Negro couple in the car tried to pretend they had
not heard, feeling embarrassed for my sake, I suppose, as
I for theirs. It seemed too grisly a joke to remind the man
of ads about his gas station's lavish *politesse*. I left.

The meeting had been transferred from its original site.
James F. Eure, Negro bishop of the Church of God in
Christ, had telephoned the local pastor, Ernest Dupree,
with instructions not to hold a political meeting in his
church. When he could not reach Dupree, he came over
himself and padlocked the door. That had begun a scurry
of all the officials who frowned on the meeting in the first
place. Now they realized that an enclosed church in Negro
territory was a far better site than open spaces near the
white zone. The Governor's office called Bishop Eure and
tried to stuff the whole affair back into his little church—
too late. New quarters had been found, and reversing the
reversal would confuse things past any hope of being sorted
out.

New quarters had been found, but not by me. I asked
local patrolmen where the meeting would be held. They
elaborately feigned ignorance, an act that should have come
naturally to them but in this case did not. They knew
where it was—they had been ordered to stay clear of it. I

was able to zero in, at last, when scattered blue turned to clots of tan: as I approached the critical sector, I found state troopers, four to a car, posted at each corner, flipping the pages of the contingency plan mimeographed last night and handed out that morning in the Cambridge armory. The eye of the storm was empty, though: even state police were held back from the actual meeting place, a spacious rickety building with a six-car garage in the rear where microphones were being rigged.

The meeting is delayed. Newsmen try to find participants they can talk to, unsuccessfully. On the long casual porch of the house, twelve children are radiant as TV cameras swivel their heads around them, pecking for the crumbs of news like absentminded birds. Five of the twelve are girls and have put on their fish-net stockings for the camera. A boy says, "Am I really on television?" A grinning man with smoky gray skin and a blue smoky voice points reporters out to them and laughs: "Want to be on TV? Go hit one of them. That'll do it."

Occasionally, a newsman tries to amble onto the porch; even, occasionally, makes it into the house—to be instantly ejected. The only one allowed to stay is the Baltimore *Sun*'s Ruth Todd, wrinkled rouged stormy petrel of race trouble in Cambridge, who came in a spongy waddle of flat heels, went up the porch and in, then stared out the screen door at all other journalists staring back.

One of the few speakers of the day to show up on time is Reverend Dupree, still padlocked out of his church. He towers, more Indian in appearance than Negro, with a deep fern-pattern of creases reaching up across his forehead like battle-scorings. "My bishop told me to get out of civil rights work; but being called as a preacher means I'm not under men but under God."

At last, escorted all around by cameras, the speakers move down the block from Gloria Richardson Dandridge's house. Most of the "big names" invited could not make it

(Gloria's new married name made one of the press services announce that Dorothy Dandridge would be present—"Posthumously?" reporters ask each other in mock surprise). The star of the show—a dim one—flew in late: Cal Brown of CORE. The local BAF is disappointed; so are the TV crews that trucked their equipment out.

The original plan was to exclude the press entirely, since the church would not hold many people. Now that the meeting has been moved into the open (only the speakers' table is inside the garage), newsmen are determined to push over what has become an interim DMZ—the choppy concrete stream of sidewalk. Others are equally determined to keep us out—foremost among them, the smoky gray man who joked with the children on the porch: his voice splinters and he has tears in his eyes at the outrage of admitting whites to exercise their subtle influence on a black struggle for black dignity. Things get tense as this little man of smoke and tears starts waving and pushing the reporters back, until a peacekeeper steps in—Eugene King, of the Baltimore County League for Human Rights. He is portly and calm and caramel, his bass voice a *continuo* to haphazard shrill voices, white and black, as he patters both sides almost imperceptibly into compromise: we are to be let in for a briefing before the talks, then granted a full press conference afterward. So in again, with strained courtesy; then out, to whoops of pleasure, after our briefing —"Get the *hell* out, honkies." It echoed (and revenged) the red-eyed defender of his gas pump's purity. Reporters giggled their way back, making light of the insults. This process so elates the speakers that they will admit us several more times during the afternoon, for the pleasure of kicking us out. We dutifully try to see the joke in this accordion act. The real joke is that "exclusion" is so empty a formality. Even back across the DMZ (which, anyway, has been creeping toward the house, onto the lawn, a few feet down the driveway), one can hear every word over the loudspeakers. It is a case of segregation for the idea's sake, black answer to the impotent white oysterer. It is "the principle of the thing."

Not that we would have missed much. The speeches run toward that black form of "camp" which Rap Brown has popularized. "Violence is as American as cherry pie" is the apotheosis of silly—of the first silliness that made cherry pie a symbol of things worth dying for. The speakers at Cambridge accepted the most spurious visions of America, and merely inverted them: "I want to grow *black* cotton, and live in a *black* plantation house, and have the *whites* picking my black cotton," one orator thundered, unconsciously putting himself back in vaudeville as a minstrel. One of the things the white community has stolen from the Negro is a sense of time, of history: they fight obsolete symbols, turning them upside down. Bojangles is now Jangbogles, and Jangbogles gave most of the speeches that day: "Shave a dog and his skin would be just the color of a white man's." We have produced a whole tribe of black Lenny Bruces.

Governor Agnew is the favorite "white devil" of the day, for ordering in his 250 troopers. While denunciations of him somnambulated through the mike, Eugene King told me they were glad to have "the state boys" in town. It is much better to deal with the troopers—or even with General Gelston's National Guard, which occupied the town for a week after Rap Brown's last appearance—than to have the local police on the scene. I would find out later that one reason General Gelston is so ready to call out the Guard in Cambridge is that this mixes local bigots in with uniformed men from around the state; it "neutralizes" them. It is one of the Guard's advantages which the Guard cannot advertise. Today the local cops are buffered from their prey, blue cushioned with tan. It is best for them not to hear their own slogans with the colors interchanged: "The white devils put all their diseases in us."

I asked King about those in the press section who clustered together, apart from journalists I knew, nursing their cameras and tape recorders. "Well," King grinned, "I know two from the Baltimore County police. I suppose the others are from the Baltimore city police and others. [Three I talked to later turned out to be state police.] The FBI is here, no doubt, but they usually have the sense not to gather with other police in plainclothes." During the crawl of words from the speakers, TV men pick up this rare sentence or that from orators who seem on the verge of saying something. Only in the police section do the tapes keep turning hour after hour, completing the dossier on each speaker. The press is blamed for turning out in such large numbers every time there is a hint of civil disturbance; but many of those lumped together with the journalists are intelligence officers, keeping their files up to date. Chiefs of police in the major cities do not need, any more, the advice given them at their last convention by Harry G. Fox, chief inspector of the Philadelphia department: "Police photographers in plainclothes, equipped with large cards indicating Press, may produce many pictures that would not otherwise be available."

Inspector Fox also recommends the use of surveillance trucks not marked as belonging to police. A telephone truck sat in the "cleared" area all that Saturday afternoon in Cambridge. The Sheriff of Cook County, Joseph Woods, described to me a technique very common now: "We have a mobile camera van on the scene; if arrests are made, we take every prisoner by and photograph him without his knowing it. This not only records what injuries he has, it identifies the arresting officer—who can develop a reluctance to admitting he arrested the man who comes into court all bandaged with supposed wounds." This proliferation of electronic and other scrutiny at every disturbance is creating a traffic problem among "press" observers. District Commander Jimmy Riordan, in charge of Chicago's Loop area where most of the city's demonstrations take place, says: "We have to keep our cameramen on the scene, to collect evidence against this 'police brutality' stuff. And now the civil rights groups have their own photographers trying to get evidence for their side." (One of these caused a stir at the Cambridge meeting by showing up with his camera mounted on a rifle stock.) A war of cameras exists, each side trying to win an engagement by filming it from the "proper" vantage point, bumping lenses in the crush of microphones and TV cables. A day or so after each demonstration, the pictures are on the police chief's desk, each of the known agitators identified, his group ties and recent travels all neatly summarized. Sheriff Woods spread a large set of prints on his desk and rattled off the record of each man in the front ranks. "When we had our riot in Maywood, I was receiving twenty-four-hour reports on the motion of known agitators in Chicago's South Side. I have one officer [on a very small force] who does nothing but correlate reports from all over on the activities of civil rights agitators." That little cluster of men in Cambridge was part of a vast army of researchers at work day and night across America.

While King politely ushered a drunk man out of the meeting, I talked with Major Thomas Smith, head of the intelligence unit of the Maryland State Police. I asked whether the National Guard was on alert today. "I'm sure they are." Is General Gelston in town? "No, but he is nearby." How near? "Quite near." On the Eastern Shore? "Quite near." If he is so near, why not work from the Cambridge armory itself? "He's afraid of getting the natives riled." Would Negro militants have to know he is here? "I mean the *white* natives." Gelston is very unpopular with Eastern Shore types, who think he is "soft" on demonstrators. In a series of clashes with rioters stretching over a five-year period, he has never killed one. A Maryland official would tell me: "They think it is a great waste for him to bring in all those guns and men and not kill off any of their niggers for them." The black movement has to denounce him too, for ritual reasons; so he was hiding from them both until he was needed—in a no-man's-land toward which lawmen are being shoved, somewhere between black and white.

Some of the black leaders claim to be students of Che Guevara's guerrilla techniques. Whatever the truth in that, they seem to have picked up their platform style from Che's interminable boss. A representative of Baltimore's Civic Action Group described how he was invited to Mayor McKeldin's office. "He asked me what we *wanted!* I like to-uh *killed* him. [Laughter.] There are Toms among us. They have to be eliminated. There goes one now." A young man walking out the driveway grins sheepishly. Actually, there has been a steady dribble in and out of listeners learning the hard way that there are more interesting things to do on a Saturday afternoon. This was not so much a "crowd" of fifty to a hundred as a drift of people by, coagulating a bit just before the speakers' stand. Children come to look at the cameras, but rarely go up the driveway. One group of small boys milled around, frothing a football clumsily up above their heads. They are bored with the words fanned or dimmed by the slight breeze, and so am I. I put out a hand for the most ambitious boy's pass; his smile sickened as he edged far around me, wondering what trick this was, nursing the ball as if it were an ally. He was a scuffed thing himself, kicked around, with invisible stitches up the scar that split him apart when he was born. He will probably live the rest of his life thinking that every white hand put out to him will hit him.

Another child came up and curved his neck around my note pad: "Hey, mister, put my name down." He was ten or eleven. I said, "Do it yourself; I'd like your autograph." The same instant bristle of fear touched his face as if with cold water. He eased away without a word. Somehow the talk of "white devils" seemed less funny (though journalists kept trying to enjoy it: "They should take this show on the road," a beefy specimen burbled).

The words are dozing toward an end. Pastor Dupree gets a big hand for the line, "They can't stereotype *me*." Cal Brown, the star, comes last; he wants to shine before the cameras, so we are admitted again to hear his speech: "The black man has been castrated." Then we are honkey'd out while preparations are made for the press conference. It is decided that this will be held at the ruins of the city's last riot, where two full blocks burned down because the volunteer fire department refused to go into the Negro section. A Negro who lost his motel in that fire committed suicide a week later. We all tramped over there, a ragged crowd, and tried to find a rallying point. On the way I asked a Negro teen-ager if he had seen the fire. He said nothing, fidgeted, mumbled a bit. "What?" I said. "Don't ask me things," he said in an angry pleading voice. When is talking informing? He was the boy with a football grown older, and scareder. The horde of half-officials leading us could not find a suitable clearing, a trustworthy mound to speak from. Blistered pipes, boilers, all the iron bowels of large buildings seemed intact; but as soon as one stepped on them, they sank and powdered ominously, umber and ocher eggshells. So everyone meandered, stepped gingerly over rubble, circled back where they began. At last the trampling settled, more from weariness than plan, by a low wall where a few cement blocks were still mortised. Brown got the cameras and said that nonviolence has not worked, then handed his calling card to reporters and squeezed out. Lemuel Chester, young BAF leader, did not like this arrangement of microphones around a CORE hub. "Why don't you ask the people who *live* here what they think? I tell you it's going to be a long hot winter in Cambridge." His followers cheer. He tells them to be back at the garage for another big meeting that night.

Seven o'clock. Most newsmen have followed Cal Brown out of town, or gone to the armory for warmth. The telephone truck is still here, though. The bogus "press" people talk more openly now about their real work. It is cold, and accommodating the old myth that Negroes rally and riot by thermometer, the crowd is drastically cut even from its thin midafternoon size. From out at the DMZ, those few who wander in the garage lights look as if they were attending a rather dim suburban cookout. Chester has promised speakers, but none show up, so he leads a singing march back toward the burnt-out block (no imagination, nowhere to go): "Ain't gonna let *Agnew* turn us around." It is like a straggly singing offshoot from the homecoming rally by a bonfire—the only such rally these kids will know, around their own kind of bonfire. After some indecisive starts, the dwindling group, mostly children, turns downtown. That is what everyone was waiting for. Radios in the carefully spaced cars crackle nervously, and Francis B. Burch, Maryland's Attorney General, hits the street equipped with a bullhorn. There is no one to use the kids, or prod them, except Chester, who is still a kid himself. They turn around.

A few blocks beyond their farthest point of penetration lies Race Street, the aptly named Berlin Wall that divides white from black, where local police have turned out for the night in their riot gear. At the first sign of trouble they take up stations along the "wall," shotguns butt-ended on their hips, barrels slanting out at the ready. One policeman got a face wound during the last riot; so now they all wear Plexiglas guards on their riot helmets. The men are strung close, at line-of-sight intervals, globed heads all moonglow white behind and on top (good targets by night), walking fishbowls, their eyes sliding like half-seen red fish as you move past them. Martian apparitions, patrolling their toy Maginot Line. White devils. Did the scruffy football-boy see this pale glow around my head when I singled him out?

These children are growing up under the gun. The skipjacks were white in the water as I drove out of town. Ghosts. Going back up the broad double road, I stopped to eat at the Holiday Inn in Easton. There were still lights on in the police barracks. I was anxious to get back across the Bay to a *real* demilitarized zone.

But is it? I was on my way to Baltimore, where two demonstrations were taking place that night and violence was expected. General Gelston, across the road from where I ate, was poised to move in either direction. He had taken up a position closer to Cambridge, since the local police there cannot handle the early stages of trouble, as Baltimore police have done. Besides, for Baltimore, there is the plan. Operation Oscar.

If you live in any major city in America, your home is mapped for defense from its own citizenry. There are elaborate arrangements being formed, codified, revised. "You name a riot contingency, and we've got a plan for it," says Frank Rizzo, the tough Philadelphia commissioner. All seventeen police divisions in New York City have separate plans, which outline such procedures as how to "freeze" an area (stop the subways from entering it, etc.). The Cleveland plan is twenty pages long. These plans are growing daily in complexity and thoroughness. If the one-way-street pattern is changed in a city, so must the plans be. Staging areas, food sources, command centers are laid out, guarded, stocked with food. On the basis of this general planning, specific orders-of-the-day are elaborated for foreseen occasions (the mimeographed sheets the troopers were thumbing in their cars at Cambridge). Police instructions for the Century Plaza demonstration in Los Angeles last summer ran to sixty-eight pages. The basic plans, jealously guarded, are kept in loose-leaf folders, so pages can be freely added or substituted. This formation of strategy goes on at several levels—in fire departments, police forces, state disaster headquarters, National Guard armories.

Then the plans must be coordinated. The Guard, following military procedure, uses classified codenames for its programs. If you live in New York, the plan is Skyhawk. In Detroit, Sundown. In the District of Columbia, Goblet Glass. In Natchez, Wet Blanket. In Baltimore, it is Oscar. All our children are growing up under the gun.

I went to talk with Major General George M. Gelston about "Oplan Oscar." He is a natty dresser, a gracious Southerner with the Tidewater dipthong "aoot" for "out," lean and military yet convivial, a *bon vivant*. (Shortly after he was made interim police commissioner for Baltimore in 1966, he hit his flashing light and made a car pull over, only to drive into its rear bumper. One imagines the man, signaled, rammed, addressed by a man in plainclothes who says, "I'm General Gelston." The temptation must have been intense to answer: "And I—Admiral Nelson." Policemen showed up, and drove their commissioner home, noting on the report of the incident that "he had been drinking." No charge was ever made against the man who had been forced to pull over.) Gelston is highly respected in military circles: not only was he a distinguished pilot in Europe during the war, he has been efficiently handling riots for the last five years. He is a riot veteran if anyone is, schooled by combat in this brand of limited warfare, though he admits himself that "the first riot I ever saw was the '63 affair in Cambridge." Riots had not, at that time, become a way of life.

He remains on good terms with the original Muse of Eastern Shore protest, Gloria Richardson (now Dandridge), who has moved to New York, but who keeps in telephone contact with the Cambridge situation, and with George. He looks back almost with nostalgia to his skirmishes with her. "This kid Chester doesn't keep in touch; and Gloria herself can't be sure of things now—she told me there would be no trouble after Rap Brown's appearance." (That was when the two blocks were burnt down and Gelston's men lost a week of work while patrolling Cambridge.) His friendliness with demonstrators infuriates the kind of reactionaries who like to see heads banged. Gelston remains unperturbed: "CORE wanted me to start making mass arrests in Baltimore, which is just a waste of time—and a dangerous one. In that sort of fracas, nightsticks get used; scalps split easily; and blood flows freely from a head wound. So I almost flat refused to make any arrests. One time they thought they had me. They left their picketing pattern and went out to sit in the street. But I knew they couldn't stand much of that concrete in ninety-degree heat, so I just routed traffic around them. They were mad as hell."

I asked about complaints that he is too friendly with leaders of the movement. "Well, it helps keep your intelligence in good order. Politicians call in a Negro lawyer or author to learn abaoot what is going on in the black community. *They* don't know. I want to have my talks with the ghetto leader, the man I'm going to face aoot on the street. Also, when a leader knows I know him and am watching him at a demonstration, he moves more cautiously. If trouble comes, he knows he can be identified for any part he had in it."

What about last Saturday in Cambridge? "Well, I was in Easton with some of my key men. I told the Governor I was moving into the neighborhood, which cuts down our reaction time by thirty minutes to an hour. We could have moved four hundred men there within an hour or so. The Governor has given me authority to take action whenever a situation gets out of hand. He feels it is better to move in ahead of time and not be needed than to wait until it's too late. It costs the state a few thousand dollars to call up the Guard, which is better than spending a few billion after your city is burnt down." *That* is what it is all about. Precisely because he is a veteran of this phenomenon called rioting, Gelston does not underestimate the task that can be given him at any moment—to save the city of Baltimore, which means to save the whole economic life of the state of Maryland. He has made it clear that when his troops move in, he will take over from the local police and run everything out of his command post. "Riots like that in Detroit are not conventional police actions. This is guerrilla warfare; these people have been learning the lesson of Vietnam. People ask why the rioters looted and burned in their own neighborhoods during the Watts and Newark and Detroit riots. But guerrillas *have* to live in a friendly environment. They slip away down alleys and back ways. If they come out, they can be cut off, isolated and captured; they know that."

Another Adjutant General who demands full control of a riot situation is Major General Almerin C. O'Hara, of New York. In a New York *Times* interview, General O'Hara said that riots have reached a level that might call for all the instruments of war, including hand grenades, recoilless rifles, bazookas. Asked about civilian instructions that might keep him from using such weapons, O'Hara answered: "Knowing Governor Rockefeller as I do, I'm sure he would not tie our hands with such instructions." He insisted that his men must not be unduly restrained: "If the military is brought in and they lose control, then what do you have left?"

General Gelston does not foresee the use of such heavy paraphernalia of war: "I only have a few tanks, and they are off in the hills of western Maryland. They might as well be in Vietnam." But he agrees that recent riots are a kind of warfare, not simple crime: "The tactics against these actions are more like city-clearing operations than the old-style 'crowd control'—except that when clearing an enemy city you don't worry much abaoot who gets killed on the other side. We have to use all the weapons of combat, yet protect the rights of innocent citizens." I asked him what approach he would have taken in riots that have occurred. "Well, in Philadelphia, the police went down streets with their normal crowd-control squadrons, and garbage cans were thrown down on them from the roofs. The first thing a *military* man thinks of is controlling the heights. I would put men on the rooftops by helicopter or with 'cherry-pickers' from the utility companies. During the Baltimore demonstrations, I kept men on the roofs, primarily as spotters then. But, say this was a riot area. [He swivels in his chair to look out of the Fifth Armory over the arabesque of crossing and underpass by the old Baltimore and Ohio station.] That brick building over there commands a view of all the rooftops in this area. I'd want a man up there right away.

"Or take Newark. Things quieted down during the second day, but on the second night a crowd gathered in front of the police station throwing bottles and rocks. The police took about as much of that as they could stand and then said 'Let's go get them.' So there was a little battle there, with clubs and everything. Now that was a perfect time to saturate the area with gas. You won't find a greater proponent of gas than I am. We've used it several times in Cambridge, with excellent results. In fact, Gloria Richardson and George Collins [editor of the Baltimore *Afro-American*] both complimented me on my tactics in using gas—and George got a pretty heavy dose. We had a classic instance of the usefulness of gas back in 1964. We had about two hundred demonstrators over here. [He draws with his finger on the desk.] Then here was a line of Guardsmen. Behind them were about a hundred and fifty press people—Cambridge is too near both Washington and Baltimore, they can send their people out in the afternoon and have them back with films for the evening news. Then there was a lunatic white fringe. We shot some gas out at the demonstrators and it drifted back over the press and the bystanders, so it cleared the whole goddam crowd at once. In fifteen minutes there was no one in the street except the Guard. You don't have riots under those conditions. And there were no dead people to embarrass us; no one had any holes in them; no kid two blocks away got hit with a stray bullet.

"CS, you know, has a great psychological effect. [CS is the military training gas, which adds to the effect of CN, or ordinary tear gas, a gagging sense of suffocation.] Once you've had a whiff of it, there's extreme reluctance to get in its way again. It gets in your lungs, makes your throat burn like hell, and you feel like you've got a steel band around your chest."

I remarked that he seems more fortunate than Adjutants General in those states which have several major cities. "Yes, we only have Baltimore to defend. But we could get some slop-over from Washington." The Maryland plan for dealing with this "slop-over" is called Tango. I asked the General about Operation Oscar (he is surprised I know the code name): "That's a plan we've had for some time. I can't give you any details of it." Is it being brought up-to-date on a regular basis? "Every week [every Tuesday, I learned] we have a meeting of intelligence personnel from the Guard, city and county police, the state troopers, the Baltimore fire department and utilities companies to coordinate our plan and stay on top of what is happening." In the past these meetings were held only in the summer. Now they are year-round. What it comes to is a twenty-four-hour watch in Baltimore—as in every major city. There is an agreement on the part of all large police departments that a riot cannot be "controlled" once it gets into full swing. Then it must run its course ("Five days," says Assistant Commissioner Nevard in New York City; "if we can keep our leaders on the street, and supplies coming, for five days, we'll outlast them—in their present state of preparedness"). The only chance the police feel they have is to snuff out the match before it hits the tinder. So every day intelligence reports cross police chiefs'

desks charting the movement of all militant leaders, pointing to suspect meetings, zeroing in on arms caches. Each
department lives with rumors, shrewd or wild, which must
be checked instantly. General Gelston, remembering his
summer as police commissioner, says, "It was all over the
place that the twenty-first of July was the day when
Baltimore would be burned down. On the thirty-first,
Washington was scheduled to go. I had people calling me
to know if it was safe to schedule a wedding in town on
a Saturday that was supposed to be 'the day.' Respectable
businessmen were sure that day was coming, tomorrow,
or next week, or sometime."

After Detroit, no police force pooh-poohs such talk.
Superintendent Conlisk of the Chicago police says, "We
had a rumor that carloads of rioters were on their way
up from Detroit. The Mayor got on television and let
everyone know that lawlessness would not be tolerated."
And then the Chicago "task force" went out on continual
cruising alert with its riot guns and helmets in the cars,
a tour of duty maintained until the end of the summer.
Some places did not stop the cruising when autumn came.
Inspector Fox of Philadelphia said to me: "It is November
now, and we have two hundred men out in buses right
this minute, besides the seven stake-out cars that patrol
all the time."

Alarmism? Perhaps. But policemen everywhere claim
they know of a hundred riots squelched for every one
that gets out of hand and into the papers. "Can we handle
riots?" is their attitude—"We do it all the time, with all
the ones you never hear of." A flutter of green intelligence
reports over the commissioners' desks has paid off in arrests
like those in New York and Philadelphia which netted
members of the Revolutionary Action Movement (RAM),
charged with possessing arsenals and plotting assassinations.
During Detroit's 1966 riot, in the Kercheval district, a
tip-off led police to men ferrying arms from Kercheval

to what would be the scene of the 1967 riot. Chief Reddin, of Los Angeles, told me: "Tom Cahill in San Francisco said that a few years ago ninety-five percent of his intelligence work was in the area of organized crime, but now ninety-five percent of it is in the area of civil rights and riots. And that is the way my department is going, too." Sometimes, of course, trust in sources of intelligence misfires—as when the Los Angeles police raided a Muslim temple last fall and found nothing there (Mayor Yorty publicly apologized to the head of the temple). But local police are still convinced the arms had been moved when news of the raid leaked out (their stike was arrested, for four whole days, like a coiled paralyzed cobra). The reliance on informers, the placing of undercover men, the meshing of intelligence networks—this task holds first priority in all cities where trouble is expected. "We want to riddle the black movement with agents the way the American Communist party is infiltrated with FBI men," one department told me. "You know the story going around about Rockwell's assassination?—that he was killed by the one remaining member of the Nazi party who was not an FBI plant?"

When old-line departments were hesitant about adding Community Relations divisions to the police force, on the grounds that policemen should not be social workers, an argument that brought some of them around was that these agencies are good for intelligence listening posts. "The troublemakers' problem," says Jimmy Riordan of the Chicago force, "is one of communication. If they want to turn out a crowd, they've got to spread the word to their own. And when they do, we'll hear." The morning I talked to him, Riordan had just arrested seventeen protesters. "Here is what I had on my desk yesterday," he said, flipping a green slip toward me. It reported that there would be trouble the next day and the department should expect to make about fifteen arrests. "One way we judge how serious they are is to find out how much money they have set aside for bail."

Other policemen showed me reports on Molotov cocktail classes, internal rivalry among the local Negro leaders, changes of strategy in the militant organizations. In Chicago, a week before the fall demonstration at the Pentagon, one inspector told me of a report they had on the number of people going to Washington from the Chicago area. In Los Angeles, a Nicaraguan student with a miniphone recorder was planted in CORE meetings. These are secret victories policemen cannot boast of, cannot normally describe or get credit for.

But a full-fledged intelligence effort is beyond the resources (both of money and of experience) available to most city departments. One intelligence officer put it this way: "The FBI can salt away agents and leave them untouched, paying them all the while, until they find out the one key bit of information, or find out there is nothing to find out. We just don't have that kind of money; our budgets are too open to public scrutiny." Still, forces like those in Los Angeles and New York—and even in Chicago—have planted undercover agents among black nationalists, paid them through cover channels like the welfare office, given them one "contact" only, and kept the secret of their police ties even from their own families. An official in Philadelphia said, "We have to arrest our own men to keep suspicion from them; and they cuss us out and complain of police brutality along with the rest of them." A Negro member of a Community Relations division complained to me: "We're supposed to be friendly with the militants, find out their gripes, open channels of communication between them and the police. But I know damn well I'm being reported by our undercover men for being *suspiciously* friendly with the radicals." Do you know who the undercover men are? "Hell no, I only find out about them when everybody does, when they blow their cover and have to withdraw." The New York department developed its undercover techniques during the war, when it scattered men along the docks and other installations to sniff out saboteurs. The same is true of port cities like San Francisco. Other large cities have trained men to infiltrate organized crime. It is a James Bond world. The ghetto, a tangle of nerve-ends anyway, breathing with close community awareness, is now probed with sensitizers of all sorts, and knows it; trades on this fact; plays with it; plants false leads. Richard Henry, head of Detroit's Malcolm X Society, says, "We have our informers too."

I asked Chief Reddin in Los Angeles if there is not a lot of duplication, of wasted manpower, in current intelligence practices. In Cambridge, for instance, there were several agencies recording and photographing the same thing. "Yes. There is duplication even within our own department. It is hard to know everything we are doing in the secret areas. But we are working on better coordination. I think eventually we will have a single nationwide clearing-house." (Soon after this interview the Justice Department recommended a computer bank of information on agitators.) Starting in January of 1968, officials of the hundred largest police departments began meetings in secrecy, under the direction of the Justice Department, to prepare for the summer of 1968. Last fall, the Major Cities Group (thirty municipalities) of the International Association of Chiefs of Police spent most of its meeting on the improvement of an intelligence net tracing the links between civil rights groups in all urban centers. Rap Brown must have the most scrutinized itinerary of any American except the President. The ghetto teems with espionage, codes, and double agents. One would think the police were readying for war. Or waging it.

2 "RIOT" OR WAR?

Fire is the strongest and oldest symbol of the crowd. . . . A crowd setting fire to something feels irresistible; so long as the fire spreads, everyone will join it and everything hostile will be destroyed.

—Elias Canetti

In 1930, when Columbus, Ohio, had its big prison riot which took 324 lives, only one reporter got into the jail—Ray Girardin. It seemed an accident in every way. So did he. He looked more like a truant schoolboy than a journalist. He had been sent there only because the city editor of the Detroit *Times*, who had been against hiring Girardin in the first place, was out of the office when a man had to be assigned to the story. Yet something in the newsman's lost-waif bearing worked magically on the prisoners. Perhaps it was the entire lack of menace in his appearance (he is short and frail). Girardin not only got into the prison; he won the freedom of it, moved in and out delivering messages—and delivering the goods to that chagrined city editor.

It was his first taste of rioting, a grisly but (in professional ways) satisfying experience. It was not, to his distress, Girardin's last riot. That occurred last summer in Detroit, when the stray-puppy reporter acted out the dream of all those cops who have wished newsmen could be in their shoes when the heat is on.

Girardin, after his debut in Columbus, became one of the legendary crime reporters of the thirties, one who moved so knowledgeably in the underworld he was accused of being part of it. But his expertise was often useful to the law: he helped solve two famous murder cases, and found the hiding place of three escaped prisoners. He also drank himself out of a marriage and into the AA. But at the end of the war he took his last drink. "He hasn't touched a drop in twenty-two years," says his friend and assistant, Detective Joe Loesche. "But don't feel sorry for him; he got his in when he was at it. He's still way ahead of you and me."

Mayor Jerome Cavanagh had the bright idea of putting Girardin's knowledge of crime to official use. If Arsène Lupin can work for the law, then why not a reformed drunkard and frequenter of low dives? In 1965, Cavanagh gambled on his newspaper friend, and the gamble seemed to work. Girardin reformed police procedures, modernized and streamlined the department, and tried to teach his cops that _criminals_ are their enemies (not Negroes, not reporters). Life seemed to be plagiarizing cheap fiction, with the happiest results. Girardin even brought his own driver, his Kato, into the police force—the man who used to take him to the scene of a story for the _Times_.

Now all that has changed. After the city's major riot, the Detroit _News_ reported that pressures were being put on Mayor Cavanagh to get rid of Girardin. These reports were routinely denied; but Girardin, soon after, announced his decision to retire—something he longs to do now, whether he was asked to or not: "You've got to bleed some, in a job like this. But my God, I've been gushing."

Police around the country interpret his departure as inevitable—like sacking the coach after a losing season. After
a riot, a scapegoat has to go; and politicians turn naturally
to their top cop when looking for a scapegoat. Usually,
police resent this built-in inequity of their trade; but their
feelings are more complex when they watch a reporter
getting his comeuppance. "He's not a policeman," Frank
Rizzo told me in Philadelphia, "he's a writer. You'll notice,
also, that he's out of a job. Maybe you can get him some
work at *Esquire*."

Girardin is certainly not like other policemen. He could
never have served in the force he commanded; he is an
inch under the minimum required height, and weighs
only 135 pounds. His face is ridged and eroded, and
when he leans back in his office chair, one has the un-
settling impression that some headhunter has shrunk Kon-
rad Adenauer's face and propped it up across the desk.
He is nervous, a pacer; in some police commissioners'
offices, special patrol calls can be heard, but Girardin has
soothing music low-pitched in the background. His speech
is sprinkled with expletives of a thirties journalist, pieties
(like "the Lord willing") of a twenties graduate from
Notre Dame—pepper and salt; the man's two sides. And
always the professional writer is watching the interim
cop: "I'm going to write a book about this experience
when I leave office in the spring. In fact, it will just about
write itself."

On the day I saw him, in November, he had just
finished Styron's *Confessions of Nat Turner*. "It has a
lot to do with what is happening in the big cities now."
And when he is not going back a hundred years in his
attempt to understand Detroit's tragedy, he goes back
thirty-seven years. "In the 1930 riot, I came out of the
prison to go to a meeting over in the state capitol. I had
just got past a National Guardsman when I heard shooting
back in the jail; so I turned around, but the Guardsman

said no one could go in. 'Hey Mack,' I said, 'I just came out. Remember?' I didn't even have a press card then; all I had was a yellow card to get me into one of Detroit's prohibition 'blind pigs.' I tried to flash that and say 'Detroit *Times*' in an important voice. But just then a scared little second lieutenant came running up waving a big .45 automatic. 'You can't go in!' he screamed. That did it: 'You're right, I can't go in,' I said, and got out of there." He was not afraid of armed prisoners—only of armed helmeted Ohio farmboys. "I went around back and got in that way. And sure enough, the next day some Guardsman leaned on his machine gun and accidentally killed three sleeping prisoners in their bunks."

"I've been on too many stories where the Guard was called up. They're always shooting their own people. [The only Guardsman killed in Detroit was shot by another member of the Guard.] I was scared stiff to bring them in. It's not their fault, and I'm forever grateful to them: they *did* help save this city. But they just don't have the training for this kind of thing. They're not used to the city, and not used to this section of the city, to the violence we see every day." Some of the Michigan Guard probably got their first glimpse of Detroit when they drove in under the riot's dark umbrellas of smoke. One Detroit newsman even says, "Hell, some of these farmboys never saw a Negro before." Girardin's comment: "Those poor kids were scared pissless; and they scared me."

Girardin didn't want the Guard; but he desperately wanted federal troops, and he couldn't have the latter without summoning the former. "We had five thousand people in the streets in no time. For a while they were multiplying a hundred times as fast as we could. They just came barreling out of those apartments. And don't fool yourself that they were in any carnival mood. I was worried about keeping my men alive in there. We ended up arresting over seven thousand people. [Girardin's total force was just over four thousand men; though seven thousand were arrested, many were allowed to stroll abroad through the curfew hours, or to loot in open daylight, because the task of arresting, booking, detaining and giving hearings to prisoners was so paralyzingly immense.] We swept the streets, but we didn't have enough manpower to secure them after the sweep. I never thought we would make arrests on that scale, but we had to. I remember, in the summer of 1965 when Bill Parker said he had to make so many arrests in Watts, I thought that was the wrong way to handle it. But I was mistaken. You have to get the troublemakers off the street."

Why was there such delay in getting federal troops? Was it the Governor's fault? "Oh, Romney's all right. He just doesn't know what he's doing." Pause; a smile—a shrug: "He's running for President. He was here in the office all the time, and he kept changing his position. First, the Vice-President called me from Minnesota; but I was out on the street. He left a message that he would call back at ten minutes after ten. The Mayor got here by then, so I said, 'Why don't you take it?' and he did. While he was speaking to him, the Governor arrived. The Mayor asked how to get federal troops, and he was told to call Ramsey Clark. But the Governor couldn't make up his mind. Why, the TV stations have him saying, even after General Throckmorton and Cy Vance had got here, that we didn't need federal troops! That's when Jerry Cavanagh said, 'Listen, I want to be a good host to you guys, but we've got to have federal troops.' That was our position right along." (Cavanagh later recalled that "we were all very civilized with each other—while the city burned.")

"They kept telling me they had two thousand National Guard, three thousand National Guard, but *we couldn't find them. They weren't on the goddam street.* We were fighting this thing ourselves without any help. I thought, 'They're going to give me this paper stuff about the National Guard, but we have to get someone we can depend on.' " The Guard, when it did get mobilized, lived up—or down—to Girardin's expectations. A Detroit *Free Press* study of all the known dead came to the conclusion that Guardsmen not only killed one of their own, and a four-year-old girl; they very likely killed a fireman too, and a visiting businesswoman from Connecticut. In the six killings for which they were clearly responsible, five victims were innocent. In another five the Guard was involved in, four were innocent. As soon as some Guardsmen rolled into town, they hit the panic button—the nearest trigger—and kept it down until they ran out of ammunition. The place was hosed over with bullets. It often began with the shooting out of street lights. "We're 'onstage' out here," they told each other; and fired their first rounds. It took some zeroing in for these marksmen to hit a light; and the long bursts unsettled other troops the next street over, who thought they heard combat around the corner. A man who rode all through the riot zone as an authorized police observer told me: "One kid came up in a jeep and started firing a .50-caliber machine gun—which can go through quarter-inch steel plating—at all the little bulbs in a store's electric sign. He only stopped when he had burned out the barrel of the gun." And his bullets, sieved through the sign, rained God knows where, probably setting off a chain reaction of response to "snipers."

But the Guard has its side of the story to tell. I heard that side in Lansing, from General Cecil Simmons, by reputation one of the toughest paratroopers in the European theater, a man who looks the way Oliver Hardy must have felt—all impressive bluster over a soldier's little bristle of moustache. But General Simmons' narrow eyes convince. "They sliced us up like baloney," he said, remember-

ing how he commanded the men who arrived first in Detroit. "The police wanted bodies. They grabbed Guardsmen as soon as they reached armories, before their units
were made up, and sent them out—two on a firetruck, this
one in a police car, that one to guard some installation."
Guardsmen were even sent to guard the city's dog pound;
headquarters had received calls threatening to turn rabid
dogs loose in the city. Policemen, busy with the tasks that
required authority to arrest, pushed the Guard off on
assignments like this—which meant that a young man
without a car or radio, without any knowledge of the
city, could get stranded, far away from any officer, without food or cigarettes, convinced (often rightly) that no
one remembered where he was.

The Guard has performed well—in Watts, Milwaukee,
Cambridge. But General Gelston, for instance, has never
let the Maryland Guard load their weapons. He is very
quick to use the lower steps of escalation—gas, bared
bayonets. But he says, "These young men are not used to
combat situations; and it is very easy for them to squeeze
off a round by accident or in panic." It was difficult to
make this rule work in Detroit, where everyone who had
a gun seemed to be using it; where Guardsmen were
scattered off to help policemen who carried (and used)
loaded guns; where men were told to load their weapons
only on the command of an officer, though many had not
seen their own officer since they arrived in the city days
before. They soon became convinced that one's life might
depend, around the next corner, on having a clip in one's
weapon—whatever that weapon might be. Vietnam has
drained all but minimal training and drill weapons from
the Guard. "I was given an M-1 rifle," one man told me,
"but I had been trained on an M-14. I had never even
seen an M-1. And when I saw one of those M-16's I
thought it was a toy." Did you load your M-1? "You bet
I did, as soon as I found someone to show me how. It

didn't matter much, since it was taken from me the next day, and I was given a .45 automatic; I had never used one of those, either. Some jeeps had no weapons in them but .30- or .50-caliber machine guns. Men shot those because they had nothing else." General Simmons lapsed as far as he ever does from Ollie supercilious to Ollie tie-fiddling: "We could not maintain integrity of the unit." Isolated from their platoons, and even from their squads, the Guard simply became lost boys in the big town carrying guns.

It was a terrifying town. I drove through the riot area with a resident of the ghetto, a teacher in one of its schools. "One learned the pulse of destruction," he said as his VW whined, methodical as a plow, up one street and down the next. "Big black clouds came from tar still smoking on the roof; then tongues shot up when the roof gave; and a steady glow showed a building was past saving." One begins counting the blanks—"instant parking lots," as they are called—but soon tires of the labor. Stores gone, like a gap in the block's teeth; corner buildings missing; single blocks leveled, occasionally two, rarely three in a row; if one side of the street has been hit, so in most cases has the other—then the looters had to run, hit a new place, syncopating their strikes against the slower rhythm of patrol cars. The wide streets were cleaned up rapidly, rubble was trucked away, blank spots tidied over. But on back streets, gutted homes had not yet been restored in late October; blackened frames stood, like rotten toothless gums; stores vomited their insides, unembarrassed, on the street. Hundreds of fires, dotted crazily about, crept toward each other like beads of quicksilver reuniting. "We had to let many buildings go," says Chief Quinlan of the fire department, "and concentrate on preventing the flames from spreading and joining."

The razed lots are very clean now; no litter on them. I would notice the same thing a week later when I teetered over Watts in a bubble helicopter—the telltale gaps were less strewn and messy than the lawns or the flat California roofs. Our cities are much better at the upkeep of ruins than of slums. The only rubbishy things in Watts were the planned monstrosities—"Watts Towers" (inverted iron ice-cream cones), scrapyards, small factories. The points where fire extracted buildings like so many teeth are sore spots the tongue skips over, unnaturally neat.

Under Detroit's mushroom cloud, nine of the Guard's tanks blundered about—one emptied its guns, unsuccessfully, at a sniper in an apartment house, then rammed the high building in taurine bewilderment. Armored personnel carriers, two-ton trucks, jeeps with gun-mounts, five Commando armored cars loaned to the city police, cruised through crowds that called them "ducks" and shouted "Quack! Quack!" as they passed. Bullets chattered in indeterminate patterns; those who survived their weave feel helpless to convey the firepower's omnipresence. They meet with incredulity and the inevitable question: if bullets were everywhere, why were so few killed?—forty-three by the official count. But none of those who lived in that rain of lead believe this figure. "We got the forty-fourth," one Guardsman told me. "We had been harassed by a sniper in a building for two nights, and were under orders not to go into the building after him. We had to stay on the street—a stupid order. The first night we sprayed the building with machine-gun fire, but he was still up there firing at us. So, on the second night, the building 'accidentally' caught fire. One stupid order made it necessary to get him with a six-hundred-thousand-dollar building instead of a sixteen-cent bullet." Needless to say, the death was unreported.

The fact that deaths were not reported can be proved even from the official statistics. One of the known victims was shot by police who drew up no report of the incident. Two other men shot by police were left to lie in a store—

other policemen found the bodies and arranged for their removal. One looter was shot by a storeowner, who left the scene and made no report to the police (which is a misdemeanor). Where combat is intense, methods of accounting for the dead tend to be casual—even when the dead are still living: a nineteen-year-old boy lay dying in a dark back yard, three people heard him groan, came to their windows, but went back to bed without doing anything. He was picked up eleven hours later, dead. Tuesday, firemen found corpses only partially destroyed in a smoldering building; the bodies had been there since Sunday, the very first victims of the riot. How many were consumed in other buildings?

After the first deaths, few Guardsmen cared to report incidents. "We were supposed to fill out all those goddam reports after every exchange of fire. You can't fight a battle and be filling out forms. We just shot and forgot. When we killed a sniper or looter, he either died in a burning building or we threw him into one. I saw at least six unreported deaths, and I was only on duty half the time in one little area." A police observer told me he had heard informed estimates that ran as high as two or three hundred deaths, and that the toll was certainly over a hundred. Congressman Conyers, of Michigan, puts the toll around a hundred. Many of those who disappeared would be unemployed, unregistered, not on welfare or relief rolls. Even among the forty-three recovered bodies there was one man for whom the police could find no address, another whose family could not be traced. Families that missed them would be unlikely to go to the police. One of the known victims died telling his family not to let the authorities know he had been shot while looting. Over 25 percent of the young Negro males in America were not tracked down for the 1960 census. Such men can hardly be said to have disappeared in the Detroit fires. They had already disappeared; they are officially invisible.

If they do not show up on the death count, they are simply keeping their record for being unrecorded.

This riot is no different from others in making it difficult to find its victims. Alfred McCloung Lee, who wrote *Race Riot* about the clash that brought federal troops to Detroit in 1943, believes the toll went higher, in that riot, than the thirty-eight recorded deaths. In 1965, Watts officially took thirty-four victims; but Captain J. Slade Delaney of the Los Angeles fire department thinks the real count should be higher. Firemen saved several looters by chopping through the roof of a store on fire; they reached them just in time. Had they come later, those men would have been gone, untraceably. Tom Hayden, in his book *Rebellion in Newark,* quotes men in police circles who think the real number of deaths was closer to forty or forty-five than the reported twenty-four.

So Detroit was worse, even, than most people realize. It was war. "We were damned lucky we didn't have a race riot," Girardin says, "where the whites take up arms, the way they did in our '43 riot. That's what I was afraid of." What prevented it? "Getting enough manpower in to make our seven thousand arrests. That kept it a police action, not an all-out struggle between the races."

Actually, there were some whites who took arms. Two of the official deaths were caused by unauthorized white civilians carrying guns into the trouble zone (they called themselves "private guards," but seem to have been without employers). This does not include the two who were killed by men defending their own stores. And many places *did* hire guards. Establishments around the battle perimeter looked for anyone who was willing to carry a gun and protect the premises. Naturally, those who volunteered for this duty were not loath to use their weapons. I talked to one private guard who shot a Negro in the stomach for refusing to raise his arms when he approached a hotel. When the National Guard came by, this man pointed out the wounded Negro, who was picked up and trucked to a hospital, no questions asked. I asked whether this was the only man he shot at. "Hell no, I emptied my Luger over and over." Did you hit anyone else? "I don't know. I shot at looters down the street, and sprayed some buildings where snipers were. I can't tell if I hit anyone; but I'm a pretty good shot." I asked Girardin if he knew of such things: "Yes, some of those private guards got pretty involved." Pretty. One of them was charged with conspiracy to murder the three men in the Algiers Motel.

This happened even though the riot was confined to the ghetto area. What would have happened if the fighting had crossed over into white neighborhoods? Girardin gave a wrinkled grimace (I had not, till then, thought his face could be further mummified): "The police would have to be neutral, fighting both sides [I remembered Gelston, hiding in Easton from both sides]—and that's an impossible task." During the Newark riot, a New York *Times* reporter saw a man patrolling a white neighborhood near the battle zone. It was 2:30 in the morning, and the man carried a shotgun—part of a neighborhood patrol, he told the reporter, waiting for "them" to spill over onto white ground. Men like Girardin were afraid that some whites would not wait for this, that marauders would enter the ghetto, leading to retaliatory raids on the part of Negroes —to all-out war by the whole inner city's population.

These were the fears in Detroit. And fear spread out from there. One ripple hit Chicago, and put the task force on the streets. But the wildest rumors were flying in other towns throughout Michigan. All the local Guard and all the state police had been sucked into Detroit. What would happen if full-scale riots broke out in Jackson, Flint, Pontiac? There actually were flareups in Saginaw (four men shot) and Grand Rapids (eight shot). Some of the badly needed state police in Detroit were stuffed into cars and sent screaming on the highway toward Grand Rapids.

In Lansing, nerves were especially taut. It is the state capital, a good place for making trouble. The Governor's headquarters, and those of the Guard and the state police, are all there, and were all undermanned. If even Baltimore, where no riots have occurred, twitches with rumors of trouble all through the summer (as Gelston found during his police days), one can imagine the atmosphere in Lansing. I talked to office workers who were afraid to drive home; to storeowners who closed early to beat the riot out of town. Property owners were clamorous for protection. They had heard that part of the Lansing fire department, like that of forty other neighboring cities, had gone to help the Detroit firemen. (Two companies even came over from Windsor, through a tunnel closed to other vehicles.)

In this crisis, the coordinator of the area's meager resources is Ingham County Sheriff Kenneth L. Preadmore. Only he has police power throughout the county. Only he can bring in every local agency to act across jurisdictional lines. This power has restored the ancient office of sheriff to a new importance in the West and the Midwest. When Chicago was alerted last summer, Sheriff Woods deputized every policeman in Cook County, to allow an instant flow of all available men toward any disturbance, all the men capable of making arrests. Even Superintendent Conlisk, the commander of ten thousand Chicago police, is now the deputy of a man with only a few hundred cops of his own. "When we had our riot in Maywood," Woods said, "Chicago's task force was poised in its cars, all drawn up in the parking lots, ready to drive toward the suburb." I asked Sheriff Woods if he meant to terminate this arrangement, made in the heat of Detroit. He said no. "They will remain my deputies as long as I am in office."

But Sheriff Preadmore, in his little office in Mason, Michigan, could not raise many bodies when Detroit had tumbled so much of the state into its earthquake. He named the possibilities, including this: "I could get the campus police from Michigan State University." Meanwhile, his men were out watching the highway from Detroit, to see if rioters would try to come into town. What if a riot did get started; what could Preadmore do? "I'm a sheriff. I can deputize anyone over eighteen years of age who will carry a gun. If I had to, I would swear out a posse. After all, I am bound by oath to enforce the law." Fine, in theory. But when the white posse rides, it is civil war.

Is that a likelihood? "I hate to say it is," Girardin answered; "but I'm afraid we're on our way to a divided society. This is a revolution, and people have not become aware of that. Certainly the President hasn't. This is not just mobs, or gang fights. It is a question of the survival of our cities. They are all in trouble—Chicago, Milwaukee, Cleveland." And, still, Detroit. Last fall Commissioner Girardin, criticized in his early days—just as General Gelston was—for being too "soft" on protest groups, asked Detroit's Common Council for nine million dollars' worth of anti-riot equipment, money to buy armored vests, machine guns, battle cars. That is a war budget; and he is a very unwarlike man.

3 "MAKING DOCTRINE"

A uniform is the best possible disguise for a man of intelligence.

—EVELYN WAUGH

The bumbling of the National Guard in Newark and Detroit led to emergency measures—"panic measures," General Gelston calls them—to improve the Guard's training for riot work. An extra thirty-two hours of such training was immediately ordered; and lesson plans came winging out from Washington. By the end of the summer, all units had begun these drills—including those which had served in Detroit. "We ran through all that crowd-control crap again," one officer told me. "Hell, I was in Detroit two weeks, and I never once saw a crowd." Hit-and-run looters, elusive snipers; the task of working with (and out of) patrol cars; the problem of being separated from one's officers for sentry duty or to "ride shotgun" on a firetruck—all the things which caused real trouble in Detroit were ignored in this "new" course of training. They had to be. The order was an act of face-saving rushed through too rapidly for the lessons of Detroit to have been absorbed.

I asked Colonel Rex Applegate, the busiest student of riot control over the last decade or so, what he thought of the Guard's new exercises. He was hunched over the white sheaf of lesson plans: "This thing was thrown together in a single weekend. I know the poor guys who were ordered to do it. They had no choice but to dip back into the old manuals and put together what they could find at the moment. But the new riots have made all the manuals obsolete—including mine." He is referring to *Crowd and Riot Control*, an adaptation to police use of his military manual on hand-to-hand combat, *Kill or Be Killed*. "I'm coming out with a new manual next year—as you can see."

We picked our way through boxes, files, folders scattered all over a rambling room in his Oregon lodge. He sleeps and works here, in a room dotted with flat islands made by planks laid on sawhorses to give him working space. Space, of all kinds, is his primary need: he is a wide-eyed large wide-shambling tall *wide* man. When he is not working, he is out fishing on the Umpqua River, which coughs decorously over shelves of rock outside his door. The river is always a gargly presence in that house, but I arrived at night, and could not see it. Rex was eager to show it to me in the morning, eager to see it himself, though he has lived on it from a child. We took his new boat out and disturbed lace patterns made in the water by a shingling rockbed. Then back into the lodge: mantel-tops and tables are forested with trophies, graceful or stout, won by Applegate in all parts of the world for marksmanship; the walls are lumpy with integuments of large fish rash enough to swim in his vicinity.

Rummaging through his files, Rex shows me riot manuals from India, France, South America. "These wartime manuals for British civil defense are still some of the best things written. Americans know so little about riots. Most parts of the world live with them and have learned to treat them as everyday matters—look at Hong Kong, and

France, and South American countries. Why, the Mexicans have a special police who do nothing but handle riots— the Granaderos, or 'grenade throwers' (from the tear-gas grenades they use). Here, we don't know what to do at each stage of a riot's growth. We wait till it gets out of hand, then roll in the machine guns. I once broke up a riot of South American students with only fourteen police-men. Ten were out on the street in uniform. I sent the other four into the crowd in plainclothes. I had cut out each one's right pants pocket and given him a tear grenade with the pin pulled. They kept the lever down with their hands until all four were scattered through the crowd, then they dropped the grenades and started yelling 'Poison gas.' The gas was invisible, no one knew where it was coming from, but they knew *something* was there—and pretty soon there was no crowd."

Ingenuity of this sort comes naturally to the only American graduate—now the only *living* graduate—of a secret British "school for assassins." He was sent there during the war, then brought back and made one of Presi-dent Roosevelt's bodyguards. "They thought if I knew how to kill him, I might know how to keep him from getting killed. I introduced the sentry use of dogs around his headquarters, and I was sitting in earshot when Roose-velt and Churchill met at Shangri-la—you should have heard them cuss each other out! My grandfather never forgave me for protecting 'that man' Roosevelt." It was an improbable assignment for an Applegate. The family traveled out the Oregon Trail under Jesse Applegate, who founded the town of Yoncolla, where Rex lives. He grew up amid the fir trees whose slow felling and pressing into plywood, chewing into paper, is the area's one industry. "That's where I killed my first bear," he said as we drove out from town to the lodge. He was given his first gun when he was six; and, after that, given a different gun each Christmas and birthday of his childhood. He has one of America's most extensive personal collections of firearms.

In the army, Colonel Applegate set up a school in close combat at Camp Ritchie, Maryland. Then, after he retired, he wrote his manual and began selling riot equipment throughout South America. He tried to move some of his products in North America, too; but no police force was interested. "I kept telling them the day would come when they would use these techniques, but no one believed me." He likes to picture himself as a lonely prophet during those years, the Billy Mitchell of riot gases; and perhaps he was. At any rate, the departments that would not listen to him turn regularly to him, now, for the latest riot tools. His out-of-the-way lodge in Oregon has become a clearing-house of information, and it is stocked with every imaginable new gimmick. When police want to know where to get a weapon, they call the Colonel. When someone thinks of a new item that could be useful in riots, they come to him too. In Miami, for instance, at the 1965 convention of police chiefs, a young man who was marketing a product called T-GASI demonstrated it to Rex, who was tremendously impressed. "It was the first real breakthrough in riot work brought about by modern research." Rex showed it to policemen he knew. T-GASI went off the public market and became an item sold only to police, called MACE. For the help he gave the young man, Rex gets a 5 percent royalty on MACE sales. "For the last three months reported, my check was seventeen thousand dollars."

I asked him if he thought the training of the Guard would improve. "Not until they make a decision whether it is to be a military unit or a riot unit. You can't have it both ways." But the federal government will not turn the Guard over to the states exclusively for use in riots, will it? "No. And they won't give cities the funds needed to train real riot units. So I don't expect to see much improvement until one of our cities gets burnt to the ground. Then they will get very interested. I've been presenting these so-called new ideas for years—at the Pentagon, to police departments—and the history is always the same. People want them one riot after they need them."

What about all the studies on riot control the government is undertaking? "They're mostly political window-dressing, like that thirty-two-hour program. You know who is in charge of getting riot information to the police? The FBI. On the eve of the '64 election, Johnson wanted to make some gesture toward the problem, and the Bureau was at hand, so he appointed them. But they're an *investigating* agency. They know no more about riots than about patrolling a beat. How many FBI men have put down riots? By mission, by training, and by their own preference they are not fitted for the task."

What about the manual they have put out for police? (*Prevention and Control of Mobs and Riots*, 1967.) "That's a good example of what I'm saying. First, it wasn't written by an FBI man at all, but by a colonel in the MP's. It reflects military thinking—masses of men and heavy weapons—when it talks about so-called practical steps. And it reflects political pressures when it says, all the time, to refrain from taking practical steps. Take this passage. [He snorts his way through a copy spiderwebbed with his notations, angry or ironic.] In the section on what to do with sit-ins and people who block traffic, it says:

> . . . the group should be advised that they are violating the law and are subject to arrest. If the activity continues arrests should be made. The use of force, police dogs, or tear gas to require the group to disperse is neither a proper police procedure nor an acceptable method of controlling demonstrators.

You can arrest them but you must do it without 'the use of force.' If they refuse to go along, or go limp, or resist, what are you supposed to do?—*wish* them into the vans?

Now the man who wrote that wasn't thinking of real police problems. He was thinking of some politician looking over his shoulder in Washington."

"Or take this part. On 'Crowd Control' it says, 'There is no firm overall rule to apply in crowd control, as there are various kinds of crowds and each presents different problems.' Then, *on the same page*, it says, 'Officers should NOT be dressed in the uniform that is sometimes associated with riot control, i.e., white helmets, boots, and similar equipment.' What happened to the advice that there are various kinds of crowds? It says there are no hard-and-fast rules, and then immediately lays one down. And that one is so silly: it says boots cannot be worn in crowd control, though motorcycle cops wear them all the time, and they are always involved in crowd control. No police force is going to take that book seriously. When it comes to naming weapons, it gives them if they are also in the military arsenal—dogs, armored vests, it's all there. But shock batons are not mentioned, nor body shields. It's just not a serious book. I don't think we can expect any government agency to come up with anything practical in the near future. They always turn these things over to the military—or to the FBI, which then calls in the military. The army (thank God) doesn't want to get involved in police work. When politicians *make* soldiers get involved, they try to get by on military precepts, without taking the time to understand police work."

I decided to test the Applegate thesis by going to the military man who is involved, all the time, in police work —General Carl C. Turner, the commanding officer of all the military police, Provost Marshall General of the United States. He is called in whenever soldiers may be needed to police civilians. He was in Selma and in Detroit, he handled the tense burial of George Lincoln Rockwell. His office is in the Main Navy Building on Constitution Avenue; but Colonel Schoultz, his "exec," turned me away with the curt notice that permission would have to be obtained from the Pentagon before I could talk with the General. He obviously did not think I would pursue this elusive favor; but I did, and about a week later I came back to Main Navy, to a Colonel Schoultz who shifted hydramatically into his smooth P-R manner, tempering with badinage the natural grumpiness of Turner, who (I was soon to find) prefers confrontations with rioters—prefers, one almost suspects, going under fire in combat—to talking with the press. "In legal language," he said at the outset, "I have too often been the 'screwee' of this process. If the newsmen are going to misquote me, then I say to hell with them. Let them make their own living without my help." There was no use trying the old line that he makes *his* living from the taxpayers, who might want, occasionally, to hear something about his performance. The line is partly phony; and Turner would not agree even with its sound part—as I learned when I said the public might resist a way of life based on extensive preparation for the control of riots. He answered: "If you're going to go by what the people want, you're never going to be prepared, because the people are not knowledgeable." It was the old military mind, still arguing that war is too important to be left to anyone *but* soldiers.

General Turner was buttressed, for his ordeal, by two public-relations types, who tried to soften any sharp edge in his answers with a *sotto voce* warble of ingratiating footnotes, amending, explaining, adding that "the General means *this*" and "what the General believes is *this*"—flute obbligato to his raspy aria. Turner, a little coiled-spring man, has a bit of Cagney syndrome, and he was obviously impatient with the frills being hung all over his words—a point on which we were in sympathy. He wears a thin almost invisible moustache of the military sort, even less substantial than General Simmons'—as if the ghost of Ollie's toothbrush had decided to haunt Stan's upper lip. He snaps his answers out: "My role in riot control? Our office 'makes doctrine' on methods and procedures." I thought the FBI was put in charge of that. "The President has made them the channel through which doctrine is disseminated; but this office *makes* the doctrine. After all, the FBI manual was written by a Military Police officer." I asked the General about a measure Commissioner Girardin thinks should be taken—the stationing of federal troops around the country for instant response to riot trouble, making the Guard's intervention unnecessary. "Definitely not! That would violate the laws of *posse comitatus* and put the country under martial law. The military should not be used against the citizenry except in extraordinary circumstances."

He does not agree, then, that riots are reaching the stage of revolution? "No, these people should not be glorified with that name. They are just *criminals*, to be arrested by police." Soft warbling from both sides: "The General means they are criminals when actually committing criminal acts," says Charlie. "Right, the General does not believe they are criminals all the time, or a criminal *class*," adds McCarthy. Turner, caught wordless in this ventriloquial rebellion, turns his head from side to side, unwilling Bergen-dummy.

I asked him for examples of his riot doctrine. "Well, good intelligence, good planning. Know what installations have to be guarded, what facilities can be called upon. A rapid show of force will prevent ninety-nine percent of these things from happening." "The General means," the General's instant (improved) playback played at me, "a police *presence*, not necessarily the use of physical force."

General Bergen, in his own voice, went on: "I think the police should have lists of all the sporting goods stores, pawn shops, and other places that sell guns; and when a riot threatens, they should go and pick up all guns in that area. This could be as routine as clapping on a curfew."

When I tried this idea out, later, on policemen, the reaction was invariably laughter. "Manpower," they would tell me, "is our main problem when a riot breaks out—finding enough bodies, rearranging our shifts, getting the right equipment and vehicles into the area. Can you imagine the time and cars and men that would be involved in going to the stores, getting someone authorized to release the stock, noting each serial number, filling out forms, loading and carting the guns? Besides, we might make it easier for the rioters—all they would have to do is capture one truck or van filled with guns, instead of going to all the stores and collecting them themselves. This is typical of the military—they think of 'pacifying' an area, confiscating hostile weapons, sending Company B to take care of it. They have masses of men to keep busy. When they come into a town, they want to preserve 'integrity of the unit.' But if we waited to have ten men for each of the jobs police are given, we would not even get *started* on a riot." The "maker of doctrine" seems to be dispensing it, around the country, to heretics, to deniers of the doctrine.

I asked the General about the tactics to be used against snipers. "Yes. There is no need to spray a building with a machine gun. The best way is to bring men up to an entry way in an Armored Personnel Carrier. Once the men are in the house, they can search the sniper out." I knew that some police departments were investing in armored cars; but many cities find them too expensive. "Oh, I was just giving an example. You don't have to have an APC. You can hang armor on a truck. Why, we have rigged up armor on our jeeps in Vietnam." Again, the military mind. There is replacement armor in one's back-up crew, and an armored division to outfit cars under battle conditions. What must police make of advice like this?

I turned the talk to a little more conventional military operation (but not, it turned out, conventional enough)—

the October twenty-first "march on the Pentagon" that climaxed Vietnam Week in 1967. General Turner was in command at the Pentagon, and I had been there to see how the giver of doctrine practiced it. The marchers on the Pentagon—35,000 of them—clustered first around the Lincoln Memorial, bees around a marble honeycomb, to hear speeches and watch the Nazi party storm the platform. Members of the National Guard were sworn in as special D.C. police and stationed, without guns, all around the city. Their mimeographed orders for this part of the operation were sixteen pages long; if serious trouble came, the plan would switch to "Goblet Glass" with the issuing of guns. When, two weeks before the march, I tried to see the D.C. Guard's commanding general, I was told he was too busy drawing up plans and tearing them down. I would have to wait till after the twenty-first.

Once the marchers went onto Memorial Bridge, the Washington police washed their hands of the affair and began to guard against any raids back toward the District. On the other side, the regular army took over, General Turner's force—MP's stationed at the Pentagon, and paratroopers specially flown in (troop helicopters still lumbered in the sky all that morning, shifting men from place to place). Here was the first flaw in the planning—the gap between escorts caused by the unpatrolled bridge. Soldiers no doubt thought that there would be no "friendly forces" who could be attacked on the bridge (they can demonstrate against the Capitol or the Pentagon, but what could they possibly do on the bridge—demonstrate against the Potomac?). Besides, troops stationed among the "hostiles" could be isolated in the swirl of people jamming the bridge. The only real observers as the line crossed were busybody helicopters, pendulous everywhere, tilting their noses, slanting low over the bridge to estimate the crowd's size and intent, take photos, look for weapons. The marchers gaped up, straining at the dim forms that moved inside those hanging bowls. It was as if the fishbowl helmets had drifted off the policemen in Cambridge, done a helicopter's reverse crab-crawl over the sky to Washington, to float there on sentry duty (our children grow up under the gun).

Trouble did come on the bridge. A chunky self-proclaimed "Freedom Fighter" had sailed earlier into the crowd at the Lincoln Memorial, flying a placard on his mast, and been buffeted by the sea of people. The placard said "Fight the Jewish Red Anarchy." Twenty policemen circled him and swam with him between them onto a slope, where they cushioned him from persistent hecklers. He said good-bye to this escort, however, when he reached the bridge; and on the bridge he kept jockeying toward the head of the march, where the cameras were. The demonstrators' own marshals tried to protect him, but he moved in a slow scuffle—punches thrown, his sign torn down, its flag on the ground, counter-demonstrators threshing to his rescue. Then one of the demonstrators held the whole march up with a demand that the police show good faith by arresting the man. The only trouble with this plan was that no police were around. Most of the stalled marchers, victims already of long speeches retarding the climax of their trip (some had crossed a continent to reach the Pentagon), thought they had been checked by the army on the other side. They chafed and fumed, while helicopters pendulumed helplessly back and forth across the dammed flood.

An attempt was made to reassemble the crowd for more speeches on the Virginia side. Then, in orderly waves, they were majestically to flow and lap at the Pentagon, and spiritually wash it away. (More literal-minded hippies planned to elevate the building with their incantations, and shake all the evil out of it.) But by this time most people were tired of speeches. The crowd frayed out across the concrete parking lot, over the slow terrace of lawn, up sharper terraces of marble that step down the Mall facade of their chosen Bastille. Those who wanted action led the way—some of them wearing helmets, gas masks, buttoned leather jackets, in the hot sun. One girl led a police dog (that's fighting fire with fire). The Hotspurs carried blunt placards: "Johnson, pull out—like your father should have." The loose crowds gathered slightly, snagged for a moment, by the hippies' sound truck, where exorcisms were being tambourined—"Out devil, out; out, devil, out; out, devil, out devil, out out *out*." Somebody had spiked the water-bucket of Old Winsockie's cheerleaders. It was a dull show, so people moved on, but the beat kept haunting them, set-ting their pace to the tambourine shiver: "Jhim-ji-ji-*jhimm*." But a quicker measure cut across this background when a small group moved over the parking lot and lawn briskly trotting, with the shout: "Hey-*hey*, viva CHE."

This Che group is the first to break the decorous, almost languorous pace so far enforced by the demonstration lead-ers; a sense of relief draws many in their bubbling wake. They, at least, seem to know what they are doing, where they are going. They have a certain discipline: their leaders wear riot helmets, carry thick "placard poles," and have bullhorns for leading the chant. They also have runners ahead, exploring approaches. The main body pauses a mo-ment when one scout comes back and waves them down a little path—one that corkscrews toward a service entrance at the Pentagon's ground level. The determined little nucleus moves on, with its vague following cloud of the curious, of journalists, the bored, those who want some action.

Federal marshals come hastening out the path, dispatched by spotters on the Pentagon roof, silhouettes that move, in miniature, confiding the lawn's activities to walkie-talkies. The marshals wear street clothes, but carry riot batons; and they have gas masks strapped to their belts. They put the batons up (small things against the flagpoles of the Che guerrillas), and try to talk the crowd to a standstill. But the bullhorns drown their words in the propulsive chant; one man breaks through and is clubbed, clumsily, superfluously, from behind—he runs into the waiting ranks of MP's. These troops move closer, and are showered with tickering branches stripped from trees beside the path. One young soldier gets a tomato in the face (he is wearing an army helmet, not the riot kind with face guard); the crowd cheers "Good shot!" "Get him again!" Military reinforcements trot down the lane, the leaders pull back, exhilarated that "our man made it in." They tear down a wire fence and slither up a weedy rise onto open lawn, still at a run along the main approach. They lead the children's crusade that jams into a dog-legged long climb of stairs at the middle Mall entrance, where, for hours, a nudging attritive war of nerves will sputter as army troops and Che's Hey-Heyers stand face-to-face daring each other to knock symbolic chips off their shoulders. Several ranks back, boys talk tough into bullhorns: "We've given enough speeches. Let's rush them!" ("Yeah, baby, you first," a man wedged in front of the bullroarer mutters.) There are plenty of troops bunched for this confrontation—rank on rank, quiet under electronic taunts. And there were ample men, also, wheeled here or there to block the ghost-circlings of the demonstration's bodyless "head." As their audience dwindled, the speakers gave up and left the platform; but, over at the goal of their march, they had a hard time finding a place to stage acts of disobedience. The redhots had outrun them, grabbed all the confrontation space. So Dave Dellinger led a swing out by the Navy Annex, where he let remaining speakers harangue the troops (no other audience was left, after all) before they were peaceably arrested. A silly huge army of men with tear gas guns met this "main force" of the "hostiles"—military thinking, so quaint. The generals kept imagining that the marchers' leaders were *leading* the march.

The trouble would come—did come—from little bands

of dissidents roving, probing, daring each other, getting progressively braver. These found a weak spot—a wide gravel road to the side stairs of the Mall verandah—guarded by only ten or so MP's. About twenty young people made a running charge through this thin rank and swept toward the one door left open on the Mall side—the door leading into the press room, with its telephones and typewriters. Girls were among the swift incursive raiders, panting and giggling with excitement. Three or four boys made it inside the press door, federal marshals flailing after them, dragging them out, bloodying their heads with batons. Other kids poured through the outer breach, once it was made. They milled at the door, receiving their wounded, denouncing the marshals. One marshal, breathless in a gray suit, his gas-mask pouch slipped around to the front like an Indian bag, knocked down a newsman in his panic; turned back toward the open door, on guard; sensed, obviously, or caught sight of a stir behind him, something moving, and spun around throwing his stick in a flaring circle—it caught a demonstrator who was just sitting down, trying to stake out territory near the doorway. The marshal's face was as gray, now, as his suit—he tried to go behind a pillar and compose himself, but the crowd had his number. "YOU'RE SCARED," they chanted, pushing around to hiss it in his face. Each time he showed his head, they stung him back with their shout. Meanwhile the doorway had been filling with helmeted faces; troops, stationed throughout the Pentagon's green corridors, had come at a trot. They paused at the door (serpent calm of gathering olive scales), bunched down the hall, and then were disgorged on order by the push of their own back line. They came out in one caterpillar rush, kicking down the stairs those who sat there clinging to ground "earned" by their charge. Journalists spilled off the eight-foot sides of the porch; I picked myself up and watched, in the shelter of the porch-side I had jumped from, the front line of soldiers come down, guns high so no one could go over them, kicking those who tried to duck under them. Beside me a man was excitedly confiding to his tape recorder that "they are hitting with the butts of their guns." My eye swept the whole front line at once. No gun was lowered; hitting would only slow the quick caterpillar thrust and tread of booted feet descending.

The troops formed a bristling circle of men to hedge demonstrators from the door. They enclosed fifteen or so journalists who could not get *inside* (the door was slammed tight as soon as the troops disgorged themselves) nor *outside* the circle. Reporters pounded in desperation for their telephones; but that entry was closed for good. The eye of the armed circle was a sad toy battlefield—glass from the light dome broken beside the door, torn black name tag from a soldier's pocket ("R. Roach"), a dangling marksmanship medal, shoddy widowed shoe, part of a sweater, a mangled child's toy looking too "planted" and literary to be true, and two large splotches of blood looking too red to be true—except that I saw it shed, from demonstrators who kept coming back, though bloodied, in a rage of oratory. Jimmy Breslin prowled about in a fit of anger at the senselessness of it all: "This is ridiculous." After about twenty minutes of isolation, we were kneaded out one at a time through the circle of soldiers—we would be in the way if gas had to be used, if more fighting occurred—and taken in single file to a back entrance where we passed one at a time once more through a tight copse of sheathed bayonets.

"That's the army," Rex Applegate laughed, when I told him how the day had gone. "They underreact, then they overreact. And those federal marshals, wandering around alone with only a stick, get shaken too easily—they swing around; they don't know how to use a baton. It should not be raised above the head. They aren't trained for this kind of work, and they aren't in ranks to give them confidence. Their only purpose in a place like that is to do the *arresting*. They should not be *fighting* too. As far as self-defense goes, they would be better off with the MACE than with a stick. You don't need training to use the MACE, and it will subdue a prisoner better than any club, without making the marshal look like a brute. There is a dare, a challenge to combat, in facing a man with a stick. But with MACE there is no test of strength, no struggle; and shedding tears does not make a martyr, the way shedding blood does.

"The military is far behind the police—who are slow enough—in learning how to handle civilian riots. The way to block access up those side stairs would have been with 'liquid banana peel' (the slippery chemical). Even if demonstrators *did* break through a line of guards, they would just flop around looking silly when they came to the concrete. The thing to do with agitators is destroy their romantic image.

"And the army should have used bullhorns for psychological purposes the way the demonstrators did. The *kids'* technique was more sophisticated than the army's. If you put a man out on the front line and let him stand there for hours being heckled, not knowing what's going on behind him, unable to talk to those beside him, with people singling him out, calling him scared, he gets psychologically isolated. But if you have the bullhorn 'talking it up,' you give the man a voice, a sense of solidarity with his unit. The secret to riot control is more the use of psychology than of brute force. You need witchcraft and voodoo."

General Turner was certain he had run "the Pentagon thing" perfectly. Why, I asked, had the approach to the one open door been so lightly guarded? "Well, a crowd like that keeps looking for a weak point, and when they couldn't find one, they made one." "We could have stopped them from getting to the door if we had wanted to use force," one of the interpreters chirped; "but then people would have got hurt." But they did get hurt when they reached the door. "You notice," General Turner goes on, "they didn't get inside the door." On the contrary, I noticed those who did. "But they got thrown right back out, didn't they? And no more got in." No; and the journalists did not get back in either. "Yes," he said, grinning at last, "I closed the door on them." Poor fellow, he does not even know who "the enemy" was. He still thinks it was *me*. What seemed at first so dispiriting—that the army has given little help to policemen in dealing with the para-military challenge of the modern riot—became oddly comforting. It seemed best that men should not be using the "doctrine" made at the Pentagon. That was, after all, the doctrine that *defended* the Pentagon on October 21, 1967.

4 LOGISTICS

*We at home were watching nothing less
than the on-the-scene telecast
of civil war.*

—BUDD SCHULBERG
ON THE WATTS RIOT.

One hopes for devices of self-correction within one's government. If the National Guard is unprepared for riot work and must turn to the FBI for help; if the FBI is unprepared for riot work and must turn to the Provost Marshall; and if the Provost Marshall does not know he is unprepared for riot work and does not turn anywhere—well, *some* higher authority should analyze what is going on, offer remedies, improve the situation. Through channels, of course.

One of several logical channels, in this case, is the President's Commission on Law Enforcement and Administration of Justice. This commission is addressing itself to the entire problem of law and order, including the handling of riots. It has, moreover, called on independent groups for the consideration of particular problems. A study on the use and development of riot weaponry was assigned by it to the Institute for Defense Analyses (IDA—which rhymes, in Washington circles, with "apple ciduh").

Although IDA's project was primarily meant to be a study of nonlethal weapons, the institute took a wide view of the question, evaluating the situations in which non-lethal weapons might be used, the available criteria for their use, the various groups that could or should use them. They considered, for instance, the FBI manual on riot control. Surely this impartial authority would point to the book's blinkered military approach to the civilian use of force? But no; it says only that the manual "represents a substantial summary of widely accepted civilian [*sic*] doctrine in the control of riots and mobs."

What, then, of the complaints about National Guard units? The group might have considered the problems Commissioner Girardin ran into when he called up the Michigan Guard—slow response, tangled lines of authority, uncertain deployment, insufficient training, disruption of the military units, isolation of individuals. Instead, the report has this to say:

> The more frequent use of the Guard, particularly at earlier stages in mass violence, may be beneficial to the effectiveness of local police forces. First, it could reduce the local requirements for manpower, equipment, and training. Secondly, it might preserve and enhance the police image in the community by allowing the Guard to absorb any transient animosities associated with riot control. In other words, the use of the Guard may eliminate any residual burden of antagonism toward the police and, hence, improve the continuing capability to deal with the more day-to-day problems.

Police find these comments almost as hilarious as General Turner's recommendation that police departments start "gun running" around the pawn shops when a riot breaks out. First, it is said that the Guard should be used "at earlier stages in mass violence." But even if Guardsmen *could* be summoned each time a tense situation arose, and even if there were no delay in the authorization of this call-up, it still takes time for men dotted about at their jobs and their homes to be reached, rallied in armories, made up into units, and transported to the scene. Meanwhile, the trouble which was great enough to merit calling them has reached a stage far from early. Saying the Guard should be used early is like saying a revolver "should" fire bazooka shells. Second, the report suggests the possibility that police departments can reduce manpower by calling on the Guard. But the test of numbers comes in the early moments of a riot, when crowds multiply much faster than policemen can—i.e., during just that time when the Guard cannot be present. Later, if the riot has reached the proportions where an army is needed, and the Guard has arrived, police resources are still strained to the limit by the task of moving these men around in a strange town, making the arrests for which soldiers have no authority (short of martial law), processing and imprisoning those arrested. For all these tasks, more policemen are needed the more soldiers there are on the scene; and for the major task, for reacting in numbers to the first hint of trouble, sheer manpower is needed long before the Guard can lend any aid.

The institute's third point is that police will not be so hated if the Guard comes in to shoot at rioters and then disappears beyond the reach of their hatred, carrying away with it any "residual antagonism" that might otherwise greet policemen the morning after. This is one of those calm official idiocies very difficult to criticize because so hard to *believe*. What entry is there into such labyrinthine innocence, what exit from it? In the first place, riots are not so much the cause of hostility as the result of it, result of the thousands of daily encounters that rub nerves raw on both sides. Even if the police could withdraw entirely from the scene of riot, turn the messy business over to the Guard, this would not noticeably affect the hostility cops will feel when they came back to their beats. And, as we have seen, the police cannot step back when the troops arrive: the police know their own city, the Guard does not. Their organizational scheme —precincts, divisions, radio bands, stationhouses, jails, courts —must be used by the Guard, under their direction. They must make arrests, process prisoners, be on hand, weeks and months later, to testify at trials. No matter how much help they get from transient mercenaries, they will be very much "in evidence," in ways that make the very term a multiple pun. Besides, the whole attempt to parcel ghetto hostilities out on a selective basis is a paper exercise, unrelated to the facts of ghetto life. The anger vented on police is a stored-up frustration with the whole "system." The cop is thought of as the Establishment's hired gun, enforcing the whole network of injustice. Complaints against the merchant who overcharges, against the finance company that sucks with a long quicksand pull on the Negro paycheck, against slumlords, against slums, against rats—all these get focused, understandably if illogically, on the walking representative of this white country's power, on the cop. Can anyone be so fatuous as to think that a new resentment, felt against Guardsmen who performed riot duty, would be fastidiously reserved for the Guard's next appearance and vented only on it; that cops who suffer for every loan shark in their area will never be connected with the soldiers who helped them police a city? Apparently some men *can* be that fatuous, in Washton. Their very language shows how little they know of ghetto life. They talk not only of "preserving" a good police image, but actually of "enhancing" it, simply by letting Guard units do the dirty work. They talk of "transient animosities" and "any residual burden of antagonism" as if the riot were an isolated moment of violence unconnected with a whole way of life.

Most policemen have the sense not to expect help from

Washington's committees. In this, at least, they agree with the most militant Negroes. Those who have had a taste of rioting can see with a glance through most reports and studies on "urban violence" (as riots are called in a language that is meant to distance and disguise reality, instilling that committee mode of thought that leads to reports like IDA's).

This does not mean that the police have been very alert in providing answers, either. They have learned their lesson slowly, inefficiently, and without coordination. Watts did not strike home to most departments as it should have. Reports from the cities that have experienced riots are often self-justifying, defensive, and prickly with political fears. Chief Reddin, in Los Angeles, says: "Girardin gave a report on the Detroit riot at the meeting of the International Chiefs of Police, but I got a very different picture—and a more useful one—from the independent observer we sent there." Los Angeles had to begin learning its lesson ahead of the others, during Watts. Many cities have yet to learn. There is no real clearing-house of information; no agreed standards for testing new products and techniques; no system for sharing the cost and results of expert evaluation. Each department lets salesmen come and go in semi-secrecy, offering the wildest and the mildest new ideas. Each department judges on its own from these sales pitches.

Yet despite this slow start in building a "doctrine" of their own, the police have an implicit orthodoxy, gradually arrived at, on the basic response to riots. I met no police official who doubted the two fundamental tenets of this creed. First, that the way to handle an incendiary situation is to blanket it, instantly, with blue; just pour the men in. They argue that this is precisely what was *not* done in the riots that got out of hand (Watts, Newark, Detroit), and that it *has* been done in cities—e.g., New York, Chicago, Philadelphia—that have had a thousand sparks but no conflagration.

The second tenet is that, once the violence starts, there should be no negotiating with ghetto leaders. Chief Parker was prevailed on, during Watts, to withdraw his men and let Negro leaders try to calm the community. But leaders, local or national, could not bring order to that outburst. Dr. King was ignored; Dick Gregory was shot. Parker regretted his move, and told police friends across the country about his angry regret. It is an article of faith in Los Angeles—recited for me, in almost the same words, by Mayor Yorty and Chief Reddin (Parker's successor)—that this was the great mistake in handling "Watts I" ("Watts II," another flare-up the next spring, was doused with men, and sizzled out). Ray Girardin criticized, early in 1967, Parker's unwillingness to work with civil rights groups. But when the Detroit riot took fire, and the Malcolm X Society offered to damp it down, Girardin ignored the offer. The risk, after Watts, is too great. The most emphatic of the many emphatic things Commissioner Frank Rizzo pounded at me on his desk in Philadelphia was this sentence: "There'll be no deals with so-called leaders in any riot."

Although everyone agrees that trouble must be blanketed, that is easier said than done. Most departments are already spread thin handling their normal assignments; and each riot brings not only its actual violence, but several further contingencies to be guarded against—which takes men. "My first thought," Girardin says, "that Sunday morning when trouble broke out in the western part of town, was that this was a diversion. The east side has our vital installations—electricity, water. It has Chrysler, and the largest pharmaceutical company, Parke-Davis. The riot broke Sunday morning, just when the heaviest shift of all, the Saturday night one, had gone off duty. Some of those who had the weekend off were at the lake or in the country. They hit us at our weakest moment." (The captain of intelligence in one major city told me he was convinced the Detroit cops were trapped into that early morning incident; it came when the force was weakest, when the "blind pig" raided was suspiciously full, the crowd suspiciously fast to gather, at dawn on a Sunday morning.) "Yet I couldn't send even the few men I had to the riot scene. I had to keep some in reserve. Then, when the men increased, so did demands. All the hospitals wanted guards, and so did every major business." (He did not mention the sentries at the dog pound.)

Even when the force is not at its lowest ebb or otherwise depleted, it is difficult to get men to the scene of a possible riot in the vehicles and with the equipment they need. When I talked to a lieutenant in the Chicago task force, he told me: "We had to learn by experience. We had all those marches in '65—thirty-two of them in a row—and the task force had to handle them. We soon learned that a hint of trouble brought us, not too many *men*, but far too many *cars*. They create congestion, and they are easy targets for the rioters. Nothing is so exciting, or gathers a crowd so fast, as a burning police car. And if men must guard their cars, they cannot be doing the job for which they came. We have to get the men into *buses*, so they can be driven to the outskirts of the trouble. The bus gives us something to take prisoners off in, too, if mass arrests are made. The bus is easier to guard than a lot of cars—you can use a single sentry, with a dog."

But as demonstrations of all sorts multiply—Philadelphia had over 500 in 1967, compared with 376 in 1966—police techniques have to become more sophisticated. Chicago police, for instance, realized that they had no back-up force that could be rapidly mobilized if they committed their task force at the first sign of trouble. Besides, it would be easy to draw the task force off with a feint, and have it, shortly afterward, struggling in vain across a clogged major city toward the real scene of trouble. So now all seven districts in Chicago have their own Tactical Units—

each a local "task force" that can deal with disturbances. Commander James Riordan told me how it works: "At a sign of trouble, I send out a call for sixteen cars, each of which must drop off one man at a precinct station where our vans are. The first eight to arrive (two arrest teams) go out in the van, with the next eight as back-up, if they are needed. We have found that arrest teams are best made up of four men, only one of them charged with the arresting. The others assist him, cordon off the area, keep spectators back, move prisoners into the van. Otherwise, we have too great a drain of men going off with the prisoners for booking. So two teams go in the van and work under a sergeant. When the task force is called in, it works in multiples of three arresting teams, under a lieutenant."

Each city is working out its own equivalent of this procedure, and establishing automatic patterns for doubled security at police headquarters and radio command posts, for the dispatching of men to key high points (water-towers, skyscrapers), for guarding utilities. Auxiliary police are being trained to come at a call and help book, fingerprint, and process the masses of men arrested. But most cities do not have as large a force as Chicago's, nor the funds needed for detailed planning. The variety of buses and vans that must be posted around the city add up to a substantial increase in the budget for cars and Black Marias. New surveillance vans, new radios, new walkie-talkies all cost money. The Pittsburgh force has an arrangement with the city transit company for emergency use of buses—the control team must drive into a riot in *rented* busses.

Colonel Applegate contends that even a complex operation like Chicago's is not sufficient. "Your task force, or mobile unit, has to be out on normal patrol, doing normal police work, with riot duty just added on. That means the unit is at least halved, at any time, because of alternating shifts, sickness, leave, vacation. And it means their riot training is squeezed into an already heavy work load. What we need is a special unit that does nothing but handle riots. People say it is a waste of manpower to have people 'doing nothing' until a riot breaks out. But they don't say that about firemen, who 'do nothing' until a fire breaks out. What the public does not realize—and most policemen don't, either—is that really effective riot technique is not learned during a week of training once a year, or even an hour of training once a week. These are highly specialized skills.

"Most police, for instance, do not really know how to use gas. They'll use too much, or too little, or the wrong kind for the situation or the locale. They do not know about its shelf-life, about each gas's limitations. And because they don't know these things, they are afraid of it themselves—afraid they will gas a sick person, that it will get out of control, drift into a hospital or onto their own men who have not been masked. There is good reason for them to be afraid. But trained gas teams, who know all about their work, would solve this."

What other functions would a riot squad have? "Well, in the riots we have had so far, communications were a real problem. The city police, the county police, the fire departments, the Guard, all have different radio bands, which will not 'net' with each other. [Illinois has attacked this problem with a statewide emergency band which will accommodate all the agencies except the military.] The riot squad could be working out new command post procedures that would cut down the difficulty of communication between all the agencies drawn in to handle a riot.

"There should be anti-sniper teams, from three to five men, each with a walkie-talkie, so they could coordinate their movements, find their man, and move in on him. People in Detroit didn't know, half the time, where the sniper really was—or if it was a sniper. But if you form a trained team, used to working together, with the time to perfect techniques for every possible contingency—all of them marksmen, with fine guns—you would solve the problem of snipers (or of barricaded gunmen, or of lunatics like the boy in the Texas tower). Just put your teams on the street and let them go hunting.

"The riot squad would always be testing and evaluating new products. It would be a corps of real professionals working out problems on a twenty-four-hour basis, yet with their work spaced so that they could respond to any alarm at once, with their whole force. This will take money —it would take federal funding, I'm sure. But it would be money well spent. Now the departments are spending money on all kinds of heavy equipment they do not know how to use, or which is not really useful. They say tanks are necessary to get in under a sniper's fire. But my team would get to a sniper without any tank."

Applegate's plan seems far-fetched—as he admits. "Oh, we think it can't happen here. They have these units in South American countries; but we will not get them in America until the first city burns to the ground." Yet we are closer to his plan than most people imagine. Special riot teams and installations are growing up around the country. Some of these are off-shoots of existing things. In Los Angeles County, a crack troop of police "mountain goats" has long existed for rescue work on California mountains and in the fires and earthquakes that plague that state. These and other services operate, with helicopters and special trucks, out of the Special Enforcement Department; and this SED's mobile command center has added a converted World War II M-8 battle car to its fleet, along with other equipment meant specially for riot work.

In Pittsburgh, I was shown into a locked room where a great stack of telephone receivers, each lying in its fetal position on a pile of umbilical cord, is kept in service, with secret numbers, for instant use. The top one is a direct line to the Governor's office. In case of a riot, all the phones would be snatched out onto desks prepared in the larger room outside, each desk assigned to a different agency—city police, sheriff's office, county police, state police, National Guard. Each desk will have four phones, a radio outlet, and four large (six feet by four feet) battle maps—the kind with clear plastic overlays on which positions can be squeaked with felt markers. One of the maps is of the whole city, the other three are of the most likely riot zones. A permanently activated riot center is coming into existence.

In Philadelphia, Commissioner Rizzo has 125 trained sharpshooters manning his seven S-Cars (S for Stakeout). They have rifles and shotguns in the cars; they cruise the city setting traps for burglars, dealing with armed men. They are now working on anti-sniper tactics, learning to shoot from helicopters; finding out which men can shoot from heights, from ladders; testing heavier guns and body armor. They resemble Applegate's "teams turned loose to hunt."

In many ways Philadelphia begins to look like the city of the future described by Colonel Applegate. It has a big force to begin with—7,000 men for a two million population (Detroit, with one and three-quarters million people, has only 4,000 police). Then, during the summer, Rizzo bought up all the vacation and furlough time, paid his men for overtime, and took as many cops as he could off other duty. He outfitted buses with air-conditioners, so police could stay in them all day, circling the city, always on call, ready to be debouched on any troubled spot. "I could have moved two thousand men in on any riot this summer, in a matter of minutes. And even without the buses we have worked out of system of 'waves' called off neighboring beats that will get five hundred men to a spot, any hour of the day or night, within ten minutes." He admits that this meant scrimping on some other activities during the summer (traffic patrol, vice investigation, etc.), and it has made summer vacation a thing of the past for policemen. And it costs money. But he thinks nothing comes before the protection of the city from a threat of total destruction. "We found and confiscated two hundred and nineteen firebombs last summer, and twelve hundred and six Molotov cocktails. Nineteen of our cars were stoned, and twenty-six firebombs were thrown."

More and more departments are agreeing with the Rizzo approach—though few have been able to get as free a hand as he is given. "If a chief of police is given permission by those in charge of the city to run a truly professional operation, he can put down riots. Of course, he must be backed up by the courts." Rizzo's free-wheeling style cheers his men on the line. The head of the police union says, "Rizzo and not City Hall is calling the shots. Rizzo is the only commissioner who has had the guts to stand up and do the job the way it is supposed to be done. When he makes a decision, the men know it's his and nobody else's. When he acts, they know he's acting on his own and didn't check with City Hall first."

This "tough line" is becoming more popular in other places, too. Police think it is about time. They argue that it was hard enough to recruit qualified men even before riots on the present scale broke out. If men are asked to face, any day, the bullets that spattered Detroit, if they are going to go up against ghetto crowds that far outnumber them, they need assurance that their commissioner has been able to lay plans, and build up a force, sufficient to back them. Elected officials, who used to want police appointees to be seen not too much and heard not at all, are loosening the reins as they watch community response to the country's Frank Rizzos. It is generally believed that Mayor James H. J. Tate was reelected in Philadelphia on the coattails of his outspoken police commissioner.

This "new style" in police work can be seen everywhere. Even a quiet leader like Superintendent Conlisk of Chicago gets in his licks—by praising Mayor Daley's firm emergency telecast during the Detroit riot, which warned anyone who was thinking of Detroit-style action that it would not be tolerated. Outside Chicago, in the county, Sheriff Joseph Woods is of the Rizzo school. "I *have* to be tough; I'm the father of eleven children. When we had our Maywood riot, I went around telling my men on the bullhorn, so all those in the streets could hear, that any rioter who raised his hand above his head would be guilty of aggravated assault and should be fired on. I also told my men to shoot carefully—we didn't have extra men to take any wounded off to hospitals. The bystanders got my message."

Frank Rizzo's father came from Italy, and became a cop. So did Frank. "We were in a minority group," he says now; "but I was brought up to respect the police." He was a tough idealistic captain, widely admired and feared, with a passion for police *competence*. (He is very proud of the fact that three armed bank robbers who made the mistake, last year, of firing on his men were all three killed before they reached the door, and no bystanders in the bank were hurt. It was all over in ten seconds.) During his days as captain, he saw a short quiet man, ironically nicknamed "Big Bill," singlehandedly bring in two holdup men and, later that same night, return two more times with prisoners. He went over and gave the man a two-day leave. Then he began working with "Rock," as he called him from that day. "Hey Rock, there are two men holed up with rifles. Shall we take them on?"

Rock—Sergeant Robert Martin—is now in charge of Rizzo's extensive pampered arsenal. He remembers his days with "the Captain" on Twelfth and Pine, in Philadelphia's "Tenderloin." "Riots? We had one there every Saturday night, and the Captain put them down. He'd face fifteen hundred men, single out the toughest loudest guy, and take him on. No one was killed; it never got out of hand.

Once we were chasing an armed robber; I was below and the Captain was climbing after him toward the roof of a building. The man who had been burglarized was out on his fire escape with a shotgun aimed at the Captain; he thought he was with the robber. I shouted that this was a police officer in plainclothes; but the man was hard of hearing. The Captain went right on. Later, when I told the deaf man what had happened, he almost fainted: 'You mean to tell me I had a gun leveled at Captain *Rizzo?*'

Rizzo is very close to his men, who know he can still do anything he might ask of them. Sergeant Martin told me: "If our police come on a barricaded gunman, they want to make an arrest in a hurry; if the Commissioner arrives on the scene, he'll probably run the door himself." After a recent drill of the Stakeout Team, one of the force's marksmen idly tried to shoot a small used tear grenade on the ground a football-field away. He tried five shots, but did not hit it. Rizzo took the rifle, elbowed it up and over a car hood, leveled, leaned into it, and pinged the can first time. Men who serve under him realize they must stay on their toes.

Rizzo gave me his philosophy, punctuated with plosive off-beat coughed throat clearings, as he leaned over a table on his large bare forearms (he had on a short-sleeved shirt, and no coat, even in November). He minces no words—though he bends some ("kuhrim'nul"): "Any big city that doesn't have enough manpower to move in fast, in numbers, is in real trouble. Of course, if you move in and just stand there, the numbers do you no good. Tell the crowd to disperse; give them fair warning. But if they don't obey, they should be taken on, immediately. The man to go after is the one that shouts 'Burn!' or 'Loot!' He has to be taken on, and taken on good, and put right in short pants." It is the old philosophy of Twelfth and Pine. "There's no place in our form of government for a riot, for insurrection, for anarchy. Nobody's going to loot a city here. Nobody's going to sack a city. That's a promise."

I asked what he thought of the argument that arrests should be avoided when tension is great, to keep from creating the fatal spark. "That's hogwash. There will be no backing off of police here. Force will be used. The real troublemakers cannot be satisfied. They take your attempts to meet their demands as a form of weakness. You have to meet them with *absolute force*."

Does that mean you are against the "minimum force necessary" concept? "No, of course not; but the minimum *necessary*. And who is to measure the least amount of force? All I can say is that the first bottle thrown, the first brick thrown, the first Molotov cocktail, the first time police are fired on, force will be met with force —and I'm tired of hearing this 'just a little bit more force.' If they fire on us, I assure you we won't use the *least* amount of force. We have to use force just as the army does. It's war. But I don't think we will ever need federal troops. We're becoming familiar with guerrilla tactics, and we have the weapons to fight a war. I consider myself an expert in guerrilla warfare, and I don't know of any problem we can't handle. We may have a riot here, but it will be the shortest riot in history."

Rizzo's hard line was still a risky one when he took it early in 1967. The tough-cop approach had been widely discredited in 1965, when the toughest cop of them all— Bill Parker—could not control the riot in Watts. But in the summer of 1967, as riots broke out elsewhere and Rizzo's city stayed pacified, other departments took up the line. Most police authorities now believe that Parker had grown overconfident, that he did not commit enough men at first because he thought his divisions could handle anything thrown at them—in short, the toughest cop was not tough enough, did not bring his whole force to bear from the very first sign of trouble.

Last summer, in New York, a list of fifteen orders was given out to patrolmen in the restive streets of Harlem ("Wear helmets if you are assigned to a hostile area . . .

be wary of rooftops where missiles may be thrown from"
[*sic*]). Asked about the opinion that police should refrain
from arrests in a tense situation, a high-ranking New York
official said his men are under orders "to arrest *anybody*
committing a crime."

In the fall of '67, departments were already beginning
preparations for the summer of '68, buying new weapons,
asking for more men. Special efforts were being made at
the sites of the '68 conventions, Miami and Chicago, where
demonstrations and harassment are expected. To prevent
the appearance of panic just before the convention, a long-
term escalation in each city was begun the preceding fall.
In Miami, Chief Walter Headley initiated a system of regular patrol by sixteen task force cars, eight canine cars, and
he backed up the move with Rizzo rhetoric: to explain
why there has been no major riot in Miami, he said, "I've
let the word filter down that when the looting starts, the
shooting starts." In Chicago, which has a large force to
begin with (10,000 men), Mayor Daley went before the
City Council in December to announce a crackdown on
crime: "If it's necessary to put five thousand more policemen on, I'll ask you for authority to put them on." The
floorleader of the Council replied: "We are providing
seven hundred policemen commencing next week. If it
requires seven thousand or seventy thousand more—whatever necessary—I back your statement to the hilt." Whatever their final number, these extra men will come in handy
during the Democratic convention, when Lyndon Johnson is counting on his good friend Richard Daley to keep
the town in order. The City Council applauded Mayor
Daley's request for more men. That act reflects a deep
change in the nation's mood, a stiffening among us of the
war spirit.

I asked Sergeant Bob Martin what effect Rizzo's kind
of leadership has on a police department. "They'd walk
through fire for him. Morale was pretty low around here

after the '64 riot. It takes the fight out of you to stand by and watch your cars burned, your friends insulted, everything you stand for being mocked. But when Rizzo came in a year ago, he gave us something to be proud of again." The admiration is mutual. One of Rizzo's main themes is the gutsiness of cops. "We have a fine bunch of men. They have made ours the lowest crime rate of any major city. Policemen are just *real brave* guys. If you want courage, go to a policeman every time." When a meeting was held to protest police brutality in the Sixth District, Rizzo went, listened, then rose: "I take exception to that. I can't listen to these tales without objecting." He pressed a woman for particulars when she accused all fifty men in the district of brutality. She could only come up with one specific act of discourtesy.

Bob Martin says, "You have to be fast in making an arrest here, or you'll get trampled by the officers behind you." There is nothing, in war, like troop morale. Nothing, for that matter, like civilian morale: during last fall's election campaign, the Philadelphia *Bulletin* ran a poll on the Commissioner, and 84 percent thought he was doing a good job. The reason? "He stops rioting here."

5 WEAPONS

. . . whose glinting armor
reeks of My Sin . . .

—JOHNIE SCOTT
(ONE OF THE *Voices of Watts*)

Seat-belted into a jet, with a level moonscape of pocked cloud below, I turned the pages and might have been circling the moon. I read, in the unearthly prose of the Institute for Defense Analyses, about new weapons, the nonlethal kind: foam your rioters, pepper them, festoon them in long swaths of chewing gum; mark them with invisible dyes, with odors undetectable except by dogs or instruments; snow them under drifts of plastic confetti, prick them with tranquilizers; rinse them down with electric sluices; stay them, with hoses.

I was on my way to see the man who has made non-lethal weapons such a promising (and lucrative) field. His name is Alan Litman. He is thirty-three years old. He invented the Chemical MACE.

At first, in the hotel room where we met, we discussed the Institute for Defense Analyses report, which had been released that day. "I think it is rather typical of a government report," he said. "It was written by a man who sat in his room and went through all the paper on the subject. Not a person from their office came to see me, or anybody else at General Ordnance [manufacturer of the MACE] or at Smith and Wesson" (which had just absorbed General Ordnance in its octopus organization). The report cites Colonel Applegate's book, and seven of his articles, but the institute did not approach him to find out about developments made since he published these works.

I asked Mr. Litman about some of the weapons discussed in the report. How about this gummy stuff that makes people adhere to each other? "We toyed with that concept. This is a skin-adhesive that has been used in surgery. But it is dangerous when used on people who have not been anesthetized. If you get stuck to yourself (your hands, say, to your face) or to another person, the stuff will hold, all right—so well, that if you panic and pull too hard, you'll tear the skin off." The report, which addressed itself especially to the limitations and dangers of each weapon, had said nothing about this. Apparently, the only "paper" on the subject dealt with the goo's non-toxicity, and with nothing else.

What about this super water-gun that shoots a pepper solution? "Very good, for seasoning food. It's too bad I don't have one of them for our steaks tonight; but I'll show it to you at the house. This is what is used as a dog repellent, you know." Later, he did smear some pepper mixture on my face (part of my general ordeal as a guinea pig that night). In twelve minutes, it began to sting. Twenty minutes later, it had raised a red welt. "Great deterrent for a man attacking you, if you can manage to run around for twelve minutes and stay out of his grasp." Why does it work on dogs? "It gets into the nostrils and mouth, and on the tongue; and has a good chance of getting in his eyes. But with a human, the nostrils and mouth are dry and not so accessible. To be effective with this, you have to score a direct hit in the eyes—which are easily shielded, or simply closed. Besides, the mixture is dangerous if too much is inhaled in the lungs.

For some reason, the Institute for Defense Analyses has shown an entirely disproportionate interest in pepper."

What about the foam? "Well, it must be light enough to be breathed. You know, at one demonstration of the use of foam for fire departments, a man slipped and fell in it, and suffocated. Even when you get it light enough to breathe at the time it is generated, it can get denser as it settles and the air evaporates. Besides, foam does not do much more than obscuring smoke, which is much easier to use." Mr. Litman did not have a high opinion of the report.

We met Alan's pretty young wife, Doris, for dinner—she is a high-school biology teacher, the co-inventor of the MACE. Then we went to the Litmans' new home, largely designed by Alan. The walls of the den resemble Colonel Applegate's, with captive arcs of rainbow on the walls. I asked about the biggest lacquered curve up there, a gun-blue slab of fish: "That's a Mako shark, one of the two big-game varieties, a shark that jumps. It will go up nine feet out of the water. It is one of the best-streamlined things in the world. See how big its tail-assembly is." He points to the large ruddering rear fins, and then to the smaller fins on his other fish. "He needs that much to stabilize him, he moves so fast."

The design of things intrigues him. We had talked, at table, of guns. "The Thompson submachine gun is a beautiful mechanism—more complex than it had to be; designed for problems that never even arose." Litman, a conservationist who disapproves of killing things—"I feel guilty, now, about those fish"—has a large collection of rare guns, whose innards he admires just as he likes the outer flow of marine line around the walls of his den.

He is not streamlined himself, but bulky, bald, looking older than he is, with a high soft voice and slightly mushy diction. He gives an almost ineffectual appearance, so diffidently offered is his wit. He is in a state of constant bewilderment—of wonder that man makes so many things so

poorly. His own inventions are scattered around the house
—an infra-red bottle warmer, a new soft-drink mixer, a
laboratory instrument for preserving absolute temperature
during experiments. He has been a consultant for Westing-
house and Wearever, turning his curiosity to commercial
use.

At the University of Pittsburgh, he wondered about
some of the assumptions made in undergraduate biology—
e.g., that all reptiles have dim intelligence because they
are, as a class, so low on the evolutionary scale. He decided to get a collection of small reptiles and slither them
through maze tests. "I have to admit," he told me, "snakes
are just doltish; but the crocodile's intelligence is extremely
underrated. The snail is pretty stupid, but the squid is
brilliant." His admiration for the crocodile's brain was
reciprocated: Ernst, the little croc he tested, became quite
friendly with him. "If you get to *know* a crocodile, you
find he's not so bad. Two of them, of course, are bad
actors—the Salt Water kind and the Nile; in fact, the
Nile crocodile may kill more men than any other animal."

Ernst is now ten years old, "still a baby," and nine feet
long. "I'll *show* you a bright crocodile," Alan said as he
led me downstairs and introduced me. Ernst beached himself on the dry end of his sloping tank, and raffishly nosed
out toward his pal, happy as a piece of driftwood ani-
mated by good booze. He opened his drawbridge jaws,
to get the soggy pouch of his neck scratched; then arched
his back, and almost purred, as Alan stroked his scales.
"He's a masterpiece of design. See this ridge? It curls the
water off around his eyes so he can get up speed without
blinding himself. And this bunch of muscle here protects
the hinges of his jaw. His teeth are all askew, you notice
—he drops and replaces them constantly. They say if you
grab a crocodile's closed snout, he can't get it open. That's
true—if you're prepared to hang on while he twists and
turns, gashing you with those bristly teeth that stick out."
It is clear, as he creates the imaginary battle, whose side

Alan is on. "He has an inner thin lid under his heavy eye-lid—it slides sideways, he can see through it, and it corrects for underwater refraction of light so he can strike accurately underwater." He works the eyebrows up and down. "Ernst is a great fisherman."

"Zoos don't know how to take care of crocodiles. They all have calcium deficiencies—did you ever notice how bad their teeth are? And they don't give them stomach gravel to help them digest." He plunks a porcelain ball down the toothy portcullis. What do you feed him? "The goldfish that don't turn bright enough to sell, and chicken necks." "Yes," said Doris, "he's probably the only kosher crocodile in existence." Doris tolerates Ernst, which is more than the ungallant reptile does for her. He is jealous—"Hate at first sight," she admits—and will strike if she gets too close.

On the other side of the room, a five-foot alligator is vying for Alan's attention. He goes over and pets it. "You can't reason with an alligator, the way you can with a crocodile. This fellow bit my arm—it took twenty-eight stitches." (I imagined the scene at the hospital: "What did *this* to you?" "An alligator bit me." "Where?" "In my basement.") Aren't you afraid of petting it now? "No, if he gets mad, his pupils will dilate. Ernst turns blue when he is mad." A third tank holds a piranha. Is it true that piranha— "Oh, most of them are frauds. Of course, there are seventeen species. I feed this one beef. But I put a frog in, and they just became good pals."

Back upstairs, Alan and Doris talk about their work in the Sierra Club and their attempts to "save the Everglades." Then they tell me how they invented MACE. A friend of Doris, another teacher, was attacked one night and beaten with a claw hammer. Alan looked into the subject of tear-gas pen guns, so Doris would be protected. But his sense of design was offended by every type he bought. "They are little firearms, but not made to fire-arm standards." He gets one and we go out on his porch to impregnate the night air with this first of many gases we will squirt and then gingerly sniff. "You see, it doesn't have an adequate safety, and the wad it blows out can be lodged in the eye. Also, the puff of gas can be blown back on you when you use it."

"I looked into the other repellents—including HALT! for dogs. But nothing seemed safe or efficient for humans. I was asking around about this, and my colleagues at Wearever told me how much aluminum tubing ALCOA was supplying to these pen guns." The result was MACE —which does not puff out a cloud, but shoots a stream of liquid, affecting only the person it hits. The stream is mostly "carrier," a swiftly evaporating stuff that gets the irritant to its target and then gets out of the way so it can work. The vapors of this off-going liquid are heavy, and slow the breathing of the man they hit. The active irritant is simply tear gas (CN); but regular tear gas affects the skin only slightly, and has its real effect on the eyes. Alan found a chemical to work with the CN (Rex Applegate swears it is Ernst-urine), breaking down the oily protective coating of the skin to let the tear gas work directly on nerve ends all over the face. This makes the victim's face feel as if it were on fire, though there is no more damage being done than CN does on the eye ducts. The action occurs immediately, the pain is severe; a man hit with the mixture closes his eyes, puts his hands to his face, and undergoes a number of psychological side-effects —disorientation, gasping, immobilization.

I had heard that MACE does not work on drunks. "Well, not if they are totally anesthetized, so that the nerve ends don't respond. But they have to be pretty far gone for that. We have had no cases where it failed to work if used properly. Some policemen think they can hit the chest, and let rising vapors do the job. That is false; you have to hit the face." Is that hard? "No, the spray-can points itself, pretty naturally, and you have a built-in tracer effect if you miss—the liquid jet. Policemen are advised to practice with our dummy models; but it takes no real skill. I suppose we could have designed it for easier aim—put a pistol grip on it; but we didn't want it to look too menacing."

Have you had many imitators? "Some. There will be more. Our major rival uses two forms of alcohol as carrier. But these hydrolize the CN, make it too soluble in water, so the cornea is not protected. That's why they have had to cut the amount of CN to the point where it is not effective. One man shot with it recently went on fighting the police. Also they leave a grease on the man which can be rubbed off on the arresting officer. And the formula is not stable enough; it eats through the can."

The MACE was not intended for riot work, but as an instrument of self-defense—first, for the woman attacked with a claw hammer; then, later, for the policeman. But it came along just when the problem of riots had made police look for new weapons, and the public was ready to accept them. A few years earlier, police had adopted a new kind of baton, with two electric poles on the end of it. Touch the end to someone's skin and press a button, a charge would leap from one to the other pole, running along the surface of the skin with a buzz that makes anyone jump. This was used to make people move when they were "going limp," hanging on to each other, refusing to clear an area. The baton was adapted from the standard cattle prod, and it was used by Southern sheriffs who did not, in other ways, show great concern for their prisoners. The "cattle prod" got hated out of most policemen's hands. So, probably, would the MACE, if it had appeared when the shock baton did. Even in 1966 it was called "paralyzing gas," and civil rights groups attempted to get it banned. But things had changed. The brutality of Southern sheriffs had been exercised with night sticks, prods, and dogs. The clemency of the North led, in Newark, in Detroit, to machine guns and tanks. Beside the machine gun the cattle prod looks very tame (and is coming back into use).

Just when new weapons became acceptable, and most of those suggested remained unfeasible, along came MACE, all ready to use in 1965. It caught on in 1966, and became wildly popular in 1967. Wildly profitable. Last August, Smith and Wesson bought the company and made Alan Litman its director of research for nonlethal weaponry —he has already come up with a new tear grenade, and is now working on a weapon for dropping a man in flight; it will release a souped-up version of the gagging gas, CS (again we go into the night to poof it around and sniff).

I asked John Campbell, Litman's partner in General Ordnance, why they sold. "It was getting too big for us to handle. We have to hire good foremen now, sales managers, researchers; and they are hard to get unless you have the stability and promotion opportunities of a big company. [Smith and Wesson is a division of Bangor-Punta Corporation.] Also, we didn't have the distributors. At first, we had people selling MACE, through some territories, out of the trunk of their cars. Smith and Wesson is one of the few companies that has established a thorough line of communication with all police departments. They have been selling them their hand guns for years. If they had wanted to drive us off the market with an imitation MACE, even an inferior one, they probably could have done it." Police buy their weapons almost on the sly. Elected officials often do not want the populace to know what new things are being bought, or tested, or looked at. At least, that is the way it has been in the past. The MACE signals a change in that respect, also: it was not bought quietly, like the cattle prods. Many departments made public demonstrations, with police shooting fellow officers, to assure the people it is harmless. This allayed some of the fear that "chemical warfare" calls up. By last fall, over three thousand departments had the MACE, and the FBI had equipped agents with it.

Although MACE is a man-to-man weapon, not originally meant for use on crowds, it has been effectively used to break up student riots (the front line of police doused the front line of hecklers, who sat down in ignominy) where, in the past, wrestling and clubbing and spraying water only invited the kids to a free-for-all. MACE will make a looter drop his spoils, where a shout does nothing and gun shots do too much. Detroit-style riots are not crowd affairs anyway. Several of those shot in Detroit were killed close up because the police feared that something in their hands might be a gun. The MACE blinds a gunman, prevents his firing even more effectively than a gun shot from a handgun would (unless it kills instantly).

Another possible use of MACE is less reassuring. "Smith and Wesson wants to put out a commercial version," Alan said. "I suppose we would have to supply a less potent mixture, to let the police keep an edge." But the idea of MACE in criminal hands is terrifying. It would be too perfect a weapon for the rapist (it takes the hands to the face, immobilizes the victim, stifles shouts in the shallow breathing, and distracts the person hit from anything but the facial pain). It would also work well in robbing stores with only one clerk—a single squirt, and the way is free to the cash register.

Smith and Wesson has moved into the riot market with great energy. It bought General Ordnance. It bought one of the two major producers of tear gas (Lake Erie Chemical). It has set up a joint subsidiary with a British company that makes obscuring smoke (an increasingly popular substitute for tear gas). It has become the distributor for Wolverine Riot Helmets (made by a man who developed the newer racing helmets). It is manufacturing the first submachine gun to be offered for nonmilitary use since the old Thompson. It has a subsidiary that deals in police radar and resuscitators. It plans to add a holster company.

Riots are big business now; and everyone is trying to

get in on the act. My interview with a deputy commissioner in Los Angeles was jockeyed in beside a test session with a mobile pancake maker—an unlikely-sounding piece of riot equipment, until one remembers the RAM group arrested in Philadelphia for planning to poison food given the police in any emergency. (Food in the riots we have had was volunteered by charitable organizations like the Salvation Army; the Philadelphia police captured enough cyanide potassium to kill sixteen hundred men if it were placed in these volunteered meals.) An oil-processing firm found that a by-product was prodigiously slippery, and the management instantly wondered if this could be used in riots. (It is now called "liquid banana peel.") The foam rolled out on airfields to cushion the touchdown of limping airplanes is offered, now, for the inundating of rioters. Barbed wire "concertinas" used to channel the run of cattle have been bought by police for barricading streets. Those who make hard baseball hats are reworking them for riot use, with radio earphones inside. The old Roman shield has come back into use, to stop thrown bottles and bricks. Sound and light are being tested—certain sound waves make men loose their bowels; other "curdling" sounds drive men from their vicinity. Light dazzles. One man has even invented a "nonlethal" flamethrower.

This search for a brand-new weapon distracts men from the fact that accepted weapons still need a great deal of work. Alan Litman says, "The level of workmanship in this area is just dumbfoundingly primitive. If household products were made as shoddily as most nonlethal weapons, they would be laughed off the market. I don't know of a single Ph.D. working in this area. Of course, the military has people at work in their laboratories, but they keep all their findings classified, and don't let police know about new developments." Alan himself has only an M.S. from the University of Pittsburgh; but he is one who very quickly got beyond the need for schooling. He does not compete, really, with the inventors of makeshift pen guns, but with the natural process that gave Ernst eyes that pop up above the water as he swims, then puts a watershed around these bulgy periscopes; a process that bunched the muscles where his jaws swing, that slid corrective lenses across his eyes for moving, hunting, down. When Alan thinks of stabilizing projectiles, he remembers the fin on the launched underwater missile hanging on his wall.

Alan's work is cut out for him. The two types of gas grenade used for years are the burning kind and the fragmenting kind. Both can start fires; be thrown back; harm bystanders. The AAI Corporation has invented a new grenade that puffs its gas out safely with a plunger; but it uses fine powder to carry the gas, and this settles quickly. True, it is easily stirred, and makes people who stroll through it do so weepingly, but this is not a deterrent to an angry assailant or rioter. There is a great deal to be done on gas grenades—and Alan has started, with one that twirls and dances when it hits.

"Gas has been used for years," Rex Applegate says. "But there is still no standard procedure, not even a standard set of gases. The army uses CS, because that is what it has been issued. It's a fine gas for use on hostiles, and for exercises—one reason it was chosen is that it makes trainees more careful about using their masks than plain CN did. But I don't think it is the first gas that should be used on civilians. The strangulation effect can make people stampede, with a Cocoanut Grove fire result. Also, many police don't have masks that will work with CS. *Obscuring smoke* is the first thing to use. It breaks up the mob's solidarity, throws the individual back on himself. Then maybe some CN in the smoke is the next step—it gives the CN a greater psychological effect if it comes in a thick blanket of smoke. Then CS could be used. There should be an escalation. But the National Guard has only one gas; most police departments have only one or two, and don't know how to use them. Dud grenades are very common—usually blamed on brief shelf-life; but lots of them began as duds." I thought the field of riot *tactics* was underdeveloped. Riot *weaponry* is at an even cruder stage.

Yet the desperation for weapons drives men into pursuit of new things before they have learned what to do with the old. Heavy weaponry is the big step now; that is what makes nonlethal weapons so acceptable. Why worry about aerosol sprays when the police are buying tanks? The cop on the beat, looking at Newark and Detroit, feels that he is outnumbered; that he will be outgunned (rioters hit the pawn shops first, where the guns are); and that the army may arrive too late next time, or not at all. The shotgun has for a long time been the accepted riot weapon: one man against an advancing crowd can hit only one at a time with his revolver; a shotgun evens the odds. But departments did not think they had to outfit every man with a riot gun. So in Newark and Detroit, police had their wives bring them their hunting guns from home—any kind of rifle or shotgun they possessed. Three of those killed in Detroit by police were shot with privately owned shoulder guns. Now the police are saying: if a shotgun is good because it evens the odds, why shouldn't an automatic rifle or machine gun be even better? These will fire faster, and fan out less, endangering fewer bystanders.

Policemen know that to call the Guard takes time; that if another city in the same state has called the Guard, they may have to work without help, or with insufficient help. The army has let police know they must prepare themselves to handle future riots without calling in federal troops every time. Since Detroit was a quasi-military engagement, the police called on to handle such things must have military equipment and techniques. Besides, even the Guard is underequipped and had to borrow some essentials from police. There are other considerations which police will not mention in public, but which must weigh with them. One is the need to keep their men from mutiny or resigning. Another is the need to preempt the battle from white guerrillas, who might follow the lead of the roving marauders in Detroit. The white community will be less quick to panic and form vigilantes if men see tanks and heavy guns ringing the ghetto, ready for war.

Whatever the justifications policemen offer, the buying of war equipment is standard procedure now, limited only by the pinch of the city budget. There is brisk competition among the makers of armored cars. The two vehicles already tested in riots were designed for war in Vietnam. Five Commandos, made by Cadillac Gage, were loaned to the Detroit police during last summer's riot. And the Chrysler patrol car was loaned to newsmen, who refused to go back under fire without protection. The Commando is an impressive car. It swims Vietnam swamps, punches cannon fire into the jungles, repels armor-piercing bullets, and air-cools the men who work its chewy machinery of treads, gears, scopes, ports, guns. In Detroit, it strolled through back yards, knocking fences down along the way, to control the T-alleys that were burrowing-paths for snipers as they sought or escaped their lairs. As the ads for the Commando note, it is a powerful "psychological deterrent." Girardin's department has asked, now, for eight Commandos of its very own, and other policemen long to pull its "ballistic armor plate" around them. Shoot the tires out, it will still run nimbly, only a bit more slowly, on the tires' thick rubber cages. A skeptic has suggested that the cars would be ideal for the next riot we have in a swamp. But the P-R men were there ahead of him, occupants of disappearing ground as the waters rise: "Think how useful it would be in a flood!" Well then, I said, what of those tall hard-running tires, meant to trot this heavy flotation bark through jungle, like so much luggage on the heads of native runners? He grew positively blissful: "Why, that's the best thing of all for doing police work. It can climb right over roadblocks or barricades. We had our car walk over a '53 Chevy for the promotion film, and it just crunched it underfoot."

Another swamp-bug, not yet bought by the army, is

yearning after the police market it could reach if it is accepted for Vietnam. This is a diamond-in-its-cushion car —an octagonal capsule of armor stuck in a floating body— made by AAI Corporation.

These three cars—Chrysler, Commando, AAI—are built for the heaviest kind of war use, and their price shows it. Other companies try to keep the price down by putting armor on a regular car chassis—e.g., the Tom Moore armored truck ($35,000); the projected Aerojet armored station wagon (with extendible pods, like some moon vehicle, to prevent the car from being tipped over); the armored delivery van (Bauer Ordnance, $12,000). The trouble with use of a regular chassis is that it is hard to make it hold enough armor to satisfy police these days.

B and H Enterprises has put its armored box on a tread —the only caterpillar vehicle in the competition. But this slows down deployment around a large city—and, even more, around a state. All these "tanks" have drawbacks of one sort or another—yet no city that can afford them seems willing to be without one. They are being surrealistically outfitted—with fire-fighting equipment, gas dispensers, foam to wash Molotov cocktails off, electric grids to repel those who try to tip them over, and all kinds of bleepers, flashers, shockers.

When I went to see the truck being assembled at Bauer Ordnance, I met first a pretty lady treasurer who nightingaled her boss's cleverness, but admitted to his one slight flaw—an attachment to his flamethrower, which (she hastened to add) would only "singe one's eyebrows." The firm's first ads for this product, she explained, had brought "an unfavorable reaction" to the use of flame for sweeping humans off the street, and she would appreciate it if I just ignored that part of their literature. We splashed through rain to the factory where Mr. Bauer himself was punching and welding and fitting his new car's armor. Perfunctorily he gazed with me in and out of holes and ports, ran his fingers over new-reamed steel; ducked under the turret and invited me into its helmet, which barely fit his own head; and then, the gleam first coming to his eye, he put a lighter again and again to a nozzle that blew it out, once, twice, three times—then it lit. But went out; on, out; cold to the Zippo's wooing; *floom*, flicker; reluctant volcano prodded to erupt. "Its fuel mixture rolls a sudden ball and then is quickly evaporated. You know [he got confidential] it will only singe your eyebrows." He played it, delightedly, around my wet shoes while I foolishly took up the challenge and child's dare, stood still, watching the boil and blue flame, getting hot but not burned. If I were barefoot, I'm sure, it would only have singed my toenails. Back over at the car itself, I noticed a gap-toothed title stuck on the standard truck hood, spelled out in the chrome alphabet of commercial makes: LOVE. The mechanics had overheard the firm's debates on euphemistic titles. ("Rescue vehicle" has so far been the favorite—that, and white paint over the olive drab, and red police lights up where the cannons used to be.)

The B and H car has a sound "curdler" that shrieks, blasts super-loud warnings and announcements, plays a horrifying soundtrack of machine-gun sounds (like cracking timbers in an earthquake movie)—"That's the old voodoo and witchcraft," says Rex Applegate, who is pushing this vehicle. When the Colonel gave a demonstration of the car in Virginia, an "underground" Washington paper suggested some basic changes for use of the car in the District of Columbia:

> The "Curdler" (electronic directional noise maker which destroys the thought train) should be replaced (for Washington use) by a series of amplified recordings of LBJ's speeches, to be played at peak volume as the tank passes through the streets. Where the "Curdler" only drives people away directly in front of its beam, the LBJ speeches will induce widespread nausea and vomiting in a four-block area in all directions from the tank. Once the initial wave of sickening sound has passed, it can be followed immedi-

ately by a recording of Hubert Humphrey patting children on the head. The monotonous thud, thud, of his hand coming down on small black heads, accompanied by the faint sounds of his happy, mindless babbling in the background, is guaranteed to drive people quickly out of their minds, thus causing them to leave the scene of the LBJ-induced vomiting and enabling the cops to hose down the streets so they will be glistening and shiny for the next wave of tourists.

An underground paper in San Francisco was less funny. It suggests that one should "roll a jellied gas bomb under the thing" and take comfort from the fact that "the XM706 in Vietnam isn't winning the war for America. Batista's armored trains didn't stop Castro. When the American government has to resort to an obscenity like this [the Bauer car], it's getting desperate."

Yes, it is. And only money sets a limit to the desperation buying. I told the Superintendent in Pittsburgh how Los Angeles County had just got hold of surplus World War II cars for only $2,500. "Where did they *get* them? I've been looking all over for them," he said. The B and H company has access to some surplus Bren Gun carriers, and is trying to outfit them as "bargain" armored cars. Cheap armor is all the cry. Old arrangements for renting bank-trucks no longer quiet constabular apprehension. High-power rifles can penetrate Brink's armor. The police remember all those rifles stolen in Detroit and never returned; remember, as well, the thousand stored Molotov cocktails in Philadelphia, and how helpless a patrol car is against such bombs; and they knew that surplus bazookas and mortars are available to militants.

They scramble for guns, both sides. Police departments now want riot shotguns for each man—to use .00 buck, a brutal charge. "The shell has nine ball bearings in it," Sheriff Woods told me. "I make sure everyone knows that." "It is like being shot with nine .38 bullets all at once," Bob Martin says in Philadelphia. The trouble with this shot is that, after a certain distance, when velocity is spent, it umbrellas out in broad fanning patterns. That is why the rifled slug is being recommended for use when facing one man. It is like shooting one of the old CO^2 cartridges used to run toy planes—but this cartridge is solid throughout, a little torpedo of lead. "It will shoot through a wall," its users boast.

Shooting through walls is the big thing now. The man at Cadillac Gage who loaned Detroit police the Commandos also showed them a Stoner gun that rips through brick buildings. "After all," he says, "a sniper can lean out, fire down, and get back before reaction time lets you shoot at him. If you just fire up, the angle of incidence is too sharp. Unless you are standing *far* off, all you'll do is riddle the ceiling. The *proper* way to shoot a sniper is through the wall." "We can knock the wall right down," says Rizzo— "Right, Rock?" "Sure, that is no problem. The trouble is: if you go through one, where does it stop? It might go through several walls and hit innocent people in other rooms. But we've solved that problem. We have a special cartridge for our .50-caliber machine gun." (It is a bullet still classified by the military, one that explodes when it hits a wall.)

"Show him our arsenal, Rock. We're proud of that." I went down, saw the hand-worked carbine Rock had made for "the Captain"; saw the racks of shotguns, carbines, rifles; saw the .50-caliber machine gun. But there is much one cannot see—all the armament out in the buses, the vans, the S Cars. A single Stakeout Car is a rolling armory; its crew cannot make ordinary car stops (for which the proper procedure is to have both officers get out of the vehicle), since they cannot risk the capture of this arsenal on wheels. Here is what the trunk of an S Car holds:

2 M-70 Winchester rifles 30/06 cal. with Bal-Var scope,
    sling, case
    200 rounds ammo

2 M-12 Winchester shotguns 12 ga. with case
    100 rounds .00 buck
     25 rounds rifled slugs
1 Thompson submachine gun .45 cal.
    500 rounds ammo
1 M-1 carbine .30 cal.
    200 rounds ammo
1 tear gas gun (Federal)
    4 Fliterite #230
    6 Speedheat #206
    6 Short RN'G #203
    4 grenades #112
    2 smoke #108
2 Scott Air-Pak masks
3 MSA gas masks (or 5 MSA masks with cases)
2 riot shields
2 riot helmets
1 field glasses
2 riot batons
1 clip board
2 riot goggles
2 bulletproof vests
1 fire extinguisher
1 half-mile light
1 equipment list
5 30-shot Thompson magazines
5 20-shot Thompson magazines
2 15-shot carbine magazines
2 30-shot carbine magazines

The Detroit force has asked for Stoner guns. Edward Stoner is the ex-marine who designed the AR-15 and the M-16, this latter the gas-operated rifle being used in Vietnam. There have been complaints of its being too finely tooled, of jamming under less than ideal conditions. But that gun was just a beginning for Stoner. Now he has the

63-A. So, during their riot, did the Detriot police. Alan Litman, the Merlin of gases, is reverent toward Ed Stoner, the gunsmiths' Merlin: "All the great gun men of the past," he says, "were inspired tinkerers, mechanics who took the existing guns and made them better—Thompson, Browning, Garand, 'Carbine' Williams. Only Stoner sat down and started from scratch, deciding what a gun should do and engineering it from the ground up. He was an aeronautical engineer, you know."

The Stoner 63-A is, at its core, a barrel inside a perforated tube, with a pistol grip on it—short, light, looking almost like a toy. Yet this is the nucleus of a whole constellation of firearms. Add a folding stock of polycarbonate, a cylinder with mounted sight, and—presto!—you have a carbine. Fold the stock, and the whole thing is not much over two feet long—ideal for paratroopers to pack with them on their jumps. Add a barrel-extension and gas cylinder, you have a full-scale rifle, semi- or fully automatic (with closed bolt), designed to fire nine hundred rounds per minute. Swing the gas cylinder down below the barrel, it is ready to fire as an open-bolt automatic. Add a belt, it becomes a light machine gun (one thousand rounds per minute). Put it on a tripod, feed it larger belts, you have a medium machine gun. Strip the stock away, lift it off its tripod, it is a gun ready for mounting in tanks or helicopters, for direct or remote-control firing. It can be changed, disassembled, built up, in a rapid blur of simple motions. It carries its own cleaning apparatus, repair tools, spare parts; yet the automatic rifle weighs only eight pounds, the machine gun is under twelve pounds.

The real power of the gun, however, is in its specially crafted bullet-action. It spews a high-velocity bullet, barely stabilized, which tears into things with a tumbling action, almost like a dum-dum bullet (the kind outlawed by the Geneva convention). I fired the gun in Warren, Michigan, and was shown an inert block of clay into which one bullet had been sent. I could stick my fist in the hole. Imagine what such a bullet will do to a man's head (lift it off), or to his chest (clean it out).

The government is still trying to decide whether the Stoner gun should be adopted in Vietnam. The Detroit police have decided. They want to carry a hundred of these out on the street next time there is a riot. Rizzo had not heard of the gun, and when I asked about it he became very curious; as I described it, his eyes lit up and he said, "Find out about this, Rock." Others, less fortunate, must buy cheap: "I've ordered twenty BAR's," Superintendent Slusser of Pittsburgh told me.

Perhaps one reason the police want so much armor is to stay on top of a generally pyramiding arms race in this country. Over three thousand guns were stolen during and just after the Detroit riot. Few have been tracked down; meanwhile, new ones are being added to the stockpile. And this arming does not stop with police and potential rioters. A Harris poll shows that over half of the American homes have guns, and over half of those who own them say they would "shoot other people in case of a riot." In Kansas City, the police are training merchants to use rifles and pistols. In some cities, private groups are allowed to police their own areas. Firemen have asked to carry arms, and a TV station's question revealed, in Baltimore, that a wide majority of those answering favored the idea of giving bus drivers guns. The need for armed protection is increasingly assumed for whole classes of people, and for private citizens. When Alan Litman, who feels guilty about the fish on his wall, drove me back to my hotel after a pleasant evening perfumed with exotic gases, we talked of Vietnam and other violence; and as he let me off, he said, "Smith and Wesson is making fifteen hundred handguns a day, and is almost a year behind on its orders. I wonder where all of those are going?"

6 GUERRILLAS

You see, there are a few more Negroes than you know about.

—LENNY BRUCE

Can peace flower from the barrel of a gun? The Reverend Albert Cleage, of the Central United Church of Christ in Detroit, thinks so: "The police, here in Detroit, are asking for nine million dollars' worth of weapons to use against us. I think every black man in America feels that the white man is just at the beginning of using genocide here. But, you know, I think genocide will come much quicker if we just get real passive. We've pretty much outlived our economic usefulness; but even so, if the white man thinks 'We're going to kill twenty-five million black people, but it's going to take fifty million white people to do it,' then he begins to wonder 'Is it worth it?' " Dr. Cleage thinks that the black community must arm itself in order to *prevent* wholesale killing—much as we stockpile atomic bombs that we may avoid using them.

But is this threat of "two white men for every black" a realistic one? After all, the odds are nine to one against the Negro, simply in terms of population—not counting the technological superiority of what Dr. Cleage calls "the white man's military establishment." The majority of those killed in past riots were Negroes. "But this will be a whole different approach," Cleage answered. "If the black man is fighting genocide, he goes out in the morning and says, 'I'm going to kill all the white men I can today, because he's going to kill me by tonight.' How are you going to kill twenty-five million of us overnight? They didn't even kill the Jews overnight in Germany—and *they* weren't resisting. *We* will be prepared. If the white man decides to destroy us, we will set out to make it the most expensive destruction of a race there has ever been in history. And I think we're capable of doing that. This is not a fight in which one tries to win." To work, a policy of preventive arming must strike a balance of terror.

I was talking with Rev. Cleage in the empty meeting hall of his large church—he sat, purring with soft eloquence, across the table from me and my escort. His features and coloring show how potent is the symbol "black"; for he is white—or, rather, the offpink brownish tint you would get if you shaved a dog. He is, externally, one of us, the enemy. His thick eyebrows and thin moustache are frosted with gray. He must, of course, wear a "natural" hair style, but it is cut so short that he looks more like a crewcut business-man, dressed conservatively for the office, than like a rev-olutionary. Still, he calls the Detroit riot the July Revolt, and thinks it is only a first stage of rebellion. He had pre-dicted, seven months before the riot, that "1967 will be a year of racial violence and conflict." When the riot broke out, on a Sunday morning, he took the pulpit to say he had been asked if he would urge his congregation to "cool it." His answer was, resoundingly, no: "Essentially, we are trying to get free, and we want justice, and we are no longer talking about love and all these other things that cluttered up people's minds for so long. We want justice and we are going to fight for it."

That is the note he has struck, over and over, in his sermons and weekly newspaper column. Reading his words, one pictures a middle-aged Stokely Carmichael, a clerical Rap Brown. He is something more serious than either—an eloquent established clergyman, not depending only on the young, a man with trained political instinct and style, attractive to radicals and moderates alike. He has been running for one office or another over the past five years; but he did not catch on fully till the riot. Even now, he offers his unbending program in the accents of a patient man soothing idiots: "The black man is an intelligence test the white man is taking. We will see just how stupid you are." His favorite words are "rational" and "reasonable."

His country-vicar style is set off by the drama of one's entry to him. His attendant ushers us into the room, a man whose "natural" is piled in Rap Brown profusion on his head—defiant cultivation of "the Brillo look." He wears the engulfing rainbow clothes of some imagined Africa domesticated. After placing us in the cleared space toward the front of the deep hall, he takes up a Secret Service position at our backs. But Reverend Cleage, when he strolls in, talks with an almost casual persuasiveness. Why, I asked, did the ghetto residents burn their own stores and homes in the riot? "In the Revolt? Those buildings were not ours. To burn down a slum-owner's shack means *he's out*. He won't come here to exploit us again. There's nothing irrational about cleaning that out of your community. The black man is only doing what the white men did in their revolution. There's nothing surprising about black men wanting to control the black community—fighting to control it, burning to control it. That's very rational." (Chief Quinlan, of the fire department, says fires were started in the offices of stores, to destroy debt records.)

Dr. Cleage preaches the Nation, the chosen people who must be kept pure of the Gentile (i.e., the white man). Perhaps that is why a visit to him is like a journey to a foreign country. I found a white man who works in the ghetto, who had the proper black connections. This contact went with his black friend on preliminary embassy, and was left at the door while the black man negotiated entry (when he came out, he apologized for leaving his fellow on the doorstep: "Oh, that's all right; it's a long-standing custom—in the South—to be denied the front door because of one's color"). The next day, this white man could conduct me to the interview; he sent his name in while we waited at the door, offered further references when we were admitted, and was surprised (as I was) by the affable Wizard we met at the center of this forbidding Oz.

I asked who would return to the ghetto once exploiters were "cleared out" by fire. "A businessman will go anywhere—to hell, if he finds a way—for profit. We are the white man's colony, the biggest richest colony he ever had, other than South Africa with the diamonds. We must teach him to invest in the ghetto just as he would in any other foreign nation." Are you in favor of colonialism then? "Neo-colonialism is all right. It's the old colonialism, still practiced in Rhodesia and South Africa, that was wrong. But neo-colonialists realize that the nation in which they invest has to have control of a business in its territory, and a just return of the profits, and full ownership over a reasonable length of time." Will men submit to these restrictions when investing in their own country? "That is better than not knowing, from one night to the next, whether one's building is going to stand. You can talk better with a businessman than with a maudlin sentimental liberal. A businessman wants to know how much money he can make —what are the risks, what are the rules. He's practical."

Dr. Cleage's opposition to the meliorist liberal, who asks what he can give the black man, was made clear just after the riot. Mayor Cavanagh appointed a typical liberal panel —the New Detroit Committee, chaired by department store owner H. L. Hudson—to decide what to do about (and for) the ghetto. It is true that the Mayor included three black nationalists on the panel (spiking the normal mixture a bit); but he did not include Dr. Cleage—and so, the evening before the committee's first meeting, a thousand black activists met at Central United Church to register their discontent with the official body. Even one of the official committee's members came to protest. The demands made that night were an unheralded preview of the action at a meeting held one month later in Chicago—the National Conference for New Politics, where a minority "Black Caucus" demanded (and got) 50 percent of the votes. In Dr. Cleage's church, on August 9, speakers said the Hudson Committee should have a black chairman, a black majority; that it should address itself merely to answering a set of black demands. Reverend Cleage summed up: "The Hudson Committee will take orders from us."

I asked Reverend Cleage, several months after that meeting, what the Hudson Committee had accomplished so far. "Oh, they are trying to cooperate with the Metropolitan Fund to merge Detroit in a six-county complex, so they can take all power from Detroit before the black people take Detroit." A typical clash between the liberal and the advocates of black power. Liberals would like to integrate the black downtown and the white suburbs; make suburban taxes available to the inner city; work together as a single metropolitan complex. The black leader watches Negro population creeping toward the 50 percent mark in city after city: "We have forty-two percent now," Cleage says of Detroit. As the balance trembles, about to turn, they foresee a last panicked rush of remaining white citizens out of town, which will leave all municipal administration to elected black officials. Reverend Cleage does not worry about tax money in that case. The cities are too vitally needed, by the surrounding countryside and by the federal government, for the nation to let them starve for funds. The black nation will have its own territory, its own government; and the white nation must come to it for the use of certain vital installations.

At this juncture there is no enemy, for a Reverend Cleage, like the liberal who tries to prevent such schism, who wants to thin the tight black centers of population out in gray larger areas. "The white man has to give us control of the cities. If he doesn't, he leaves us no alternative but violence. There's no other choice. The white man is still toying with the idea that there's a third possibility, but he's just wasting time." Who stands in your way? "The white liberal is the most difficult person to get rid of. He's got emotion, prestige, and everything tied up in _his_ leadership. Moynihan is almost a classic pattern of what happens to the liberal. His study tries to show that the black community is sick; but the black community is not as sick as the white community." If the black community is sick, it must still be ministered to by white surgeons, like Moynihan—which Cleage resents. He thinks that Moynihan, losing support among the black, has turned to the Right for support, to hold on to his power: "Moynihan issued a statement that the time had come when white liberals and white bigots had to get together." (He is referring to a speech before the ADA calling for a "politics of stability" that could unite all moderates, Left and Right, to prevent the growth of terrorism in America.) Moynihan has become a favorite target of black militants, ever since his Department of Labor report on _The Negro Family_ appeared. Rap Brown, speaking on educational TV, said that, while black men take care of their own problems, white men should begin "to talk about civilization of Lyndon Johnson, to talk about civilization of James O. Eastland, to talk about the civilization of Patrick Moynihan."

The other enemy, after the liberal, is "the Negro" (carefully to be distinguished from "the black man"): "The Uncle Tom is a traitor," Rev. Cleage told me, "and what have you white men always done, historically, to traitors? That's right, killed them." It is all said in the mildest know-your-candidate manner.

It is difficult to judge how much of the black community shares Rev. Cleage's strategy for municipal takeover. But it is perfectly clear that ghetto residents vibrate to his rhetoric of pride, of self-respect; and appreciate his denunciation of injustices they have experienced. During the riot, three unarmed black men were killed in the Algiers Motel, and a policeman is now under indictment for their murder. The pent-up anger over what the black community calls this "massacre" was given vent in Dr. Cleage's church when a "People's Tribunal" tried the policeman *in absentia*. It was the new Nation conducting its first case of genocide, in truest Bertrand Russell style: the jury was made up of people like Mrs. Rose Parker, who began the historic Montgomery boycott when she stayed in the front of a bus, and Negro novelist John Killens. Two jurymen were white—but they were members of People Against Racism, a group meant to "civilize the whites."

The church itself is a symbol of black aspiration. Near the place where the Detroit riot began, there is a streetside all-white statue of Jesus, on the grounds of a Catholic seminary. During the revolt, the face and hands and feet of this statue were painted black—in imitation of the black Jesus and black Mary whose portraits flank the entrance to Dr. Cleage's church. Inside the church, there is a full-length picture of the black Madonna, unveiled last Easter Sunday in connection with a call for a "Black Christian Nationalist Movement." The artist, Glanton Dowdell, was one of those convicted of carrying arms in the Kercheval riot of 1966. The muted Dr. Cleage and his flaming attendant Zulu took us from picture to picture in a little pilgrimage. There is a stylized tear in the eyes of Jesus and Mary, who look as if some Negro Norman Rockwell had confected them. The exotic bodyguard relaxes his monosyllabic rigidity before the Madonna, and whispers, to no one in particular: "She's so beautiful—in a way that does not make you think of sex." It is the voice of the new chivalry, of ascetic knights who ride unseen through the TV films of looting and arson, elite warriors of this new Nation. This is the "new Negro" who appeared first in the disciplined secret cadres of the Muslims, but who is found now in a hundred groups, religious or mystical in character. I asked Dr. Cleage what part religion plays in the movement. "Religion is the heart and core and center of the black Nation. We were misled in religion just like we were in history and culture. Most black people in America didn't know till a few years ago that the black culture in Africa was far superior to the white man's in Europe. All our education has been miseducation. For thousands of years, when the white man in Europe was a barbarian, black people in Africa had a philosophy, astronomy, science, libraries. But black people didn't know it because white men didn't put it in the book."

"The same way with religion—religion was given to us by the slave masters in the South, and they gave us a lie. Christianity is essentially the religion of the black Messiah. The Jewish nation started with Abraham, who came from the Chaldean portion, and those were Arabs (as known today). When Abraham left, as the father of Israel, he mixed with all of the peoples of the Mediterranean and Africa. The Old Testament is a record of this racial mixture that took place in building the black nation, Israel. Moses was married to a black woman. Joseph was married to an Egyptian. There were no white people in the area until the development of the Greco-Roman period, as an imperialism. So there was no way in the world Jesus could have been white."

Is Jesus the Savior of white people as well as black? "That's up to the white men. I preach about the Nation— the black Nation, the black Messiah. Jesus was building on the Old Testament. The first three Gospels of the New Testament are historical. The Gospel of John is later, as are the epistles of the Apostle Paul. Paul was trying to relate the Gospels of the black Messiah to the white Gentile world. Jesus had no conception of anything the Apostle Paul talked about—the whole universalism, brotherhood. White people preach that; they very seldom turn to the Old Testament—all black preachers, even the most ignorant black preachers, preach primarily out of the Old Testament and the first three Gospels. There has always been a definite division between the Christianity of black people and the Christianity of white people—Jesus on the one side, and Paul on the other."

Does God reject the white man? "God created man in his own image (that's the Bible again), and does not want that dignity to be torn down; so he would be concerned with those who are oppressed. It is divine justice, knowledge, wisdom that Jesus would come to the black people." Yet you say the white man is sick. Has God abandoned him in his sickness? "I think Paul has a message for white people. They need that kind of religion. They have to believe in universalism because they are the oppressors. They're concerned about guilt. God is concerned about my oppression, and he tells me what to do to get rid of it. He's concerned about your guilt, and he tells you what to do to get rid of that. White people need the epistles of Paul. But for a black man to believe in the universal brotherhood of man is demeaning, and psychologically destroys him. The oppressed need one thing, and the oppressor another. Now God in his infinite wisdom has seen fit to give them both what they need. For black people to say 'We're going to love everybody' would destroy us; it would be a sickness with us."

A wild emblematic history—but not so wild as the Muslim version of Genesis (with its reverse Manichaeism, angelic-black quenching the devil-white); and look what that theory has wrought, in terms of pride and discipline. For fighting against the odds, nothing is so practical as mysticism, the luminous simplicities, the inner (illogical) light.

Dr. Cleage's homiletic style echoes, across a century, the pulpit corruscations of another violent divine: "Sharps rifles are a greater moral agency than the Bible." On the eve of civil war, Henry Ward Beecher stirred congregations with words like that; and when rifles were sent into Kentucky to aid abolitionist guerrillas, the crates were marked "Bibles." Beecher's Bibles became the term for all guns sent to support abolition, and the sermons grew more and more "unwordly": "Let no man pray that John Brown be spared! Let Virginia make him a martyr!" When war came, Beecher made his home an armory for Union ordnance.

Dr. Cleage is very interested in guerrilla tactics. When I asked him about the Mayor's request for nine million dollars in riot weapons, he said, "Their arms are not going to be any more effective here than in Vietnam. You don't need superior arms. The Blacks are not going to be stupid enough to throw bricks at tanks." Though his rhetoric is Northern abolitionist, his strategy is the dreamy Southern one, of light rapid marauders against the clumsy machine. The new secessionist is a creature of the forlorn hope, like the Confederate leaders; and, like them, he can call his doubting Lees back to defend him, drawn against their better judgment by the ties of blood. If the Cleage minority issues a call to arms, many in the black majority will feel they must support "the brothers." As Dr. Cleage puts it: "There are no 'good darkies' anymore." And after predicting the riots in 1967, he has this to say about 1968: "Next summer, if conditions are the same, we'll probably have rebellion in the streets just as we did this year."

Using my interview with Cleage as passport, I tried to travel a bit in his Nation. I went to The Easel, a black art shop, and asked if I might interview the owner: "I am the owner, and I have set a policy for all the CCAC that we will not talk to white newsmen." But Dr. Cleage talked to me. "I won't." The CCAC—Citywide Citizens Action Committee—is the group that was set up at the meeting which protested the Hudson Committee's makeup.

I went to Vaughn's Bookstore, the literary center of the revolution—raided several times, I had heard, during the riot, and doused by firemen though it was not on fire. I asked about this; was told that these things happened. The lady in charge at the moment (Vaughn himself is at a meeting with Dr. Cleage) is minimally courteous, but uncommunicative. The shop is busy, its patrons well-dressed, the black intelligentsia. The book selection is extraordinary, covering all aspects of the race struggle in America and the accession to power of African nations. The books lean toward hagiography (with Malcolm X and Muhammad Ali as the leading heroes) and is trans-racial only in one sense: all advocates of revolution are admitted to the Pantheon. Che Guevara is here, and Mao (in an expensive multi-volumed edition), Fidel and Regis Debray. There are special offprints of a *National Guardian* article on last summer's rebellion—"The Birth of a Nation"—written by local celebrities (and CCAC members) Grace and James Boggs. Readers are given the choice of four Michigan Negro newspapers, one of which, the *Inner City Voice*, publishes items like this:

POLICE INHUMANITY

Mrs. Jacqueline M. was dragged from her apartment by white police officers and taken to the 10th Precinct. Policemen inside the station fondled the private parts of her body, while she was in the interrogation room. They put their hands underneath her clothing, then ripped off the top part of her pajamas. Police photographers took pictures of her exposed body, while various white police officers posed holding her breasts. Then they ripped off the lower part of her pajamas (she had been sleeping when the police broke into her apartment), and made her stand nude in the middle of the room for over an hour.

This operation, which involved considerable manpower, was supposed to have taken place during the riot, when police were desperate to get more men on the streets and newsmen swarmed in precinct stations. Devils do not bother with minor things like strategy; and mystics see devils in the light of revelation, not of logic. One *Free Press* reporter who worked on the exposé of police and National Guard responsibility in the forty-three reported deaths said that rumored luridities were accepted without question throughout the ghetto—e.g., that all three men in the Algiers Motel had their genitals shot off.

I asked Detroit's police commissioner, Ray Girardin, if he thought Cleage the most influential of the militant black leaders. "He is getting the attention now; but I think Cleage is being used by smarter people behind him. The ones who do what planning there is in these blow-ups are highly intelligent. We had them under surveillance all through the riot."

I asked him about the two brothers who founded the Malcolm X Society, Milton and Richard Henry. "They are very bright and eloquent." The two leaders offered to stop the revolt if Mayor Cavanagh would meet their demands (withdrawal of troops, amnesty, funds for co-ops, etc.). Milton Henry, a lawyer, also served as prosecuting attorney at Reverend Cleage's "People's Tribunal." He is a Muslim, and was an associate of Malcolm X. Milton was out of town when I visited Detroit, so I called on Richard Henry, who prefers his post-slave name, a Swahili one, Imari. He was reluctant to be interviewed, after an NBC special on the Detroit riot. "Bill Matney double-crossed me, and we're old friends; we used to work on the same newspaper together." Matney, a Negro reporter, obtained interviews with black militants around Detroit who claimed that some of the rioting and arson during the riot was planned. I thought Imari might resent this contention, but that was not the case: "Oh, some of the burning was planned; in fact, a lot of it was. They hit sections in teams." What he re-sented were the factual inaccuracies (that a mysterious white man runs the black movement); and, even more, that no militant was allowed to express the separatist *philosophy* on the screen. I assured him that was precisely what I would report on, and was allowed to visit him at his home.

Imari, or "Rick," as he is known to his old friends, lives in a large home sparsely furnished. His teen-age daughter was watching television with her friends; they got bundled out of the front room into the kitchen when I came. The home is middle-class in appearance; Henry has a govern-ment job, as a technical writer. He is slight, wears a long-suffering smile, and breathes soft laughter through his words. Bitterness has reached, in him, the point of last-hope gaiety, a what-is-there-to-lose enjoyment of the risks he lives with. He agrees with Cleage that genocide may be just around the corner. "Black men are finally beginning to realize that the cowboy-and-Indians shows on TV are about *us*. The people who count—the army, the police, who do the fighting for the white community—have reached the conclusion that society is not going to adjust to what the black militants want, so they are preparing for war against the militants." I asked if this war apparatus has intelligence units inside the black movement. "Oh yes; anytime they want to get us, they know where we are and what our habits are. But"—the laughter is breathing as he says it—"I just read recently that the head of one section of British intelligence turned out to be a double agent. Remember this, too: black people realize that they have dues to pay, and most are paying them."

Imari differs from Cleage on several crucial points. For one thing, Cleage still tries to negotiate with the white establishment for black take-over of the city. "People don't realize how easy it would be to get along with the CCAC, with Cleage and the Boggses. They keep telling the white man 'You have one last chance.' They want a cut of the action. And, you know, Johnson is just like the Mafia. When he sees we're getting more and more votes, he says, 'OK, boys, I'll give you a cut of the action.' But our people have suffered too much to join the exploiters now." If the Negro were given his share of the action, wouldn't that stop exploitation? "No, the nation's whole policy is racist. We are willing to have good relations with the white Communists. We give milk to Yugoslavia and train their pilots. We trade with Russia. But we look toward Asian Communists and get all upset. That's how bad our racism is. South Africa has systematized the dehumanization of my people. Yet look at all the money we pour into that country. The ghetto is only one of the colonies America exploits. It's too late for Johnson to bribe us. We don't want to be co-exploiters. We want to do away with exploitation."

A more serious point of difference with Reverend Cleage —whose church, nonetheless, Imari and his Muslim brother attend—is on the matter of the revolution's base. Cleage and the CCAC argue that the Northern city is the logical base. Imari just laughs at this, as a romantic conception. "We can hold the cities *gloriously*—for about a week. Then we run out of food." He looks to the South, to counties with a black majority. He waits, not for black mayors to be elected in the cities, but for black sheriffs in the South. "We will have to fight, and we must do it from positions of strength. We must be ready so that, under pressure, we won't have random immigrants, but organized *movements* to the South. When push comes to shove, it will be there." But isn't that condemning yourself to a backward agrarian base? "Did Israel start as a backward country? We'll take the best things with us." Grin—"We'll take nuclear power" —fading to a speculative look: "If you go to Alaska, you don't go and live like the Eskimos. Besides, the separatists are developing their international contacts, to get the moral weight of the rest of the world on our side, and their economic weight, and military weight. All we have to be is strong enough to hold off military attack on our Southern bastions until these foreign alliances can exercise their influence." How will they do that? "For instance, the deterrent effect of Chinese nuclear subs in the Gulf of Mexico. With those at our back, we can feel safe." (Does China promise these things, I wondered? And wondered, Why not? Promises are not performance.)

But the odds remain stacked against the enclaves Imari would retire to. His troops would be fighting the most powerful military establishment in the world. "It's a good thing nobody told the Viet Cong that. The government's resources are unlimited. Ours are only limited. But we don't have to move until we want to. That's how the odds get evened. Oh, we might end up with too little too late. In a real military engagement, success is never assured. Maybe we will be like the Sitting Bulls and Crazy Horses, and you all will build some monuments to us and say 'Weren't they wonderful Indians? Too bad we killed them all.' That's horse racing."

Like Dr. Cleage, Imari hopes the black community can make it too expensive for the whites to extirpate them, once they dig in at their base. If this stand-off is reached, he thinks the government can be persuaded to grant the land base as a matter of reparation for criminal injury inflicted during centuries of enslavement and discrimination. "If a mail truck hits a dog in the street, the government will acknowledge it committed a tort and pay injuries. Yet the government killed us and kept us slaves for years. West Germany paid reparation to the new state of Israel, not to individuals—and did this for crimes committed by an earlier government, the Nazis."

The concept of reparation is catching on in the black community, and even being put into practice. In Plainfield, New Jersey, an enterprising young ghetto dweller has collected money from local merchants as a return from their exploitatory profits. He leads a Youth for Action Movement which claims seventy-five "drilled black cadets." He led a nineteen-day boycott against a tavern which, he claims (the tavern owner denies it), refused to house one of his collection boxes. This boycott, which cost the tavern an estimated $9,000, was mentioned when he went to other owners and asked for cash donations. The machinery is old—that of the protection racket. But the justification is new—"reparations."

Many in Detroit think Rev. Cleage the most extreme voice of the black community. But Imari makes his softly voiced position seem moderate (Cleage forgoes, for one thing, the hope of Chinese subs). The day after I visited Imari, I asked the Negro reporter who best knows the ghetto—Joseph Strickland of the Detroit *News*—if the Henrys are the most extreme leaders in the black community. "No, Jack E. Wilson makes them sound moderate." Can I see him? "No, he won't talk to the white press." I had to content myself with the moderation of Imari, whose forthcoming book is called *War in America*, and who told me: "There are two kinds of people in this country who realize that the race war has in fact begun—they are the white military establishment including the local police, and the black militant leaders."

But, unfortunately, others share his belief that it is a matter of all-out war. In Detroit itself, for instance, these white groups agree with him—Post #375 of the American Legion, United War Veterans for Defense of the United States Constitution, Breakthrough, Citizens Committee for Civil Defense, Detroit Police and Firemen Association for Public Safety, and Chaldean Committee for Preservation of Liberty. These are the groups that put out a joint statement which says of the riot: "Are YOU READY NOW to PREPARE YOURSELF for the NEXT ONE? Or will you be forced to stand helplessly by because you were

UNprepared to defend your home or neighborhood against bands of armed terrorists who will murder the men and rape the women?" To make sure that people are prepared, Breakthrough holds meetings at various halls (Veterans of Foreign Wars, Knights of Columbus, the City-County Building) where spokesmen for the National Rifle Association demonstrate and recommend guns—the model for home defense shoots one hundred yards and should have two hundred rounds "per family."

The head of Breakthrough, Donald Lobsinger, has staged his own demonstrations, broken up civil rights meetings and marches, and disrupted interfaith church services. Three days before the riot started, Breakthrough picketed a Catholic church with signs calling the priest inside a traitor, a "red ally." The group puts out a leaflet describing survival kits for the next riot (food, medicine, vitamins, etc.); it recommends that its members join the General Douglas MacArthur Shooting Club. During the riot, its leaflets offered a $1,000 reward for the arrest and conviction of Mayor Cavanagh on a charge of "criminal negligence" in putting down the riot—the white equivalent of Dr. Cleage's "People's Tribunal." Cleage is very much aware of the arming on the other side: "The ranges of the shooting clubs are packed; the city is way behind in processing gun registrations. So, naturally, any black man who can get hold of a gun is getting hold of it." I got an eery confirmation of his words on the very day he spoke them. Out at Imari's house the phone rang, my host went and spoke into it briefly, and returned shaking his head in comic exasperation: "That idiot! He just said he could get us two carbines if I had seventeen dollars. *He* should know my phone is tapped."

7 THE CULT OF REVOLUTION

Aside from the basic African dialects,
I would try to learn Chinese, because
it looks as if Chinese will be the most
powerful political language of the future.

—MALCOLM X

Frank Rizzo, in Philadelphia, says "I consider my-self an expert in guerrilla warfare." Our children, growing up under the gun, can claim a similar expertise. *Time* maga-zine recently reported that the favorite books in the stu-dent bookstore at Columbia University are Frantz Fanon's *The Wretched of the Earth*, Stokely Carmichael's *Black Power*, Regis Debray's *Revolution in the Revolution* and *The Autobiography of Malcolm X*. The store sounds remarkably like Vaughn's Bookstore in the Detroit ghetto.

The civil rights movement and student rebelliousness have had a close relationship ever since Mario Savio came back for the fall term at Berkeley after a summer in Mis-sissippi. Today, the two movements go separate paths—there were few young Negroes in the Pentagon march. But they share a common literature and set of principles; each side has a romantic interest in the "practical" techniques of revolution. They defend each other's stands, as similar in inspiration. And they give more than indirect support to each other. Arthur Waskow, white fellow at the Institute for Policy Studies in Washington, defended Detroit snipers as acting in self-defense, and he called on the New Left to "insist that under no conditions should the local police, state militia or federal forces be permitted to act like a conquering army."

The Black Caucus at the National Conference for New Politics showed how much leverage one set of revolutionaries can exert on another. A less publicized example occurred around the same time at the Third Annual Conference of Socialist Scholars, in New York. A Black Power panel was chaired by James Boggs, from Dr. Cleage's CCAC, who said the rioting would spread to twenty cities next summer, taking the form of "military battles." He demanded aid from the socialist scholars: "There is no in-between. You are either with the revolution or you are not." Ivanhoe Donaldson, one of the steering committee of the New Politics meeting in Chicago a week before, said, "In Detroit we defeated the police and the National Guard," and in the future "two or three Detroits at the same time are going to pin down the American forces" (a possibility that Hanson Baldwin had considered earlier in the year, in a New York *Times* article). On the subject of sabotage, Donaldson said, "There's a Chase Manhattan Bank at 125th Street in this town. We're trying to get jobs in a bank we ought to destroy." Boggs said, as he left the session: "They put us down in Cleveland last time. But I'm riding out to the airport with someone who's going to tell me how we can fix it so they won't be able to next time."

A leaflet passed out at this meeting offered, for seven dollars, a seven-week course in "Demonstration Defense." It presents various techniques for countering police moves, whether on foot or horse, with clubs or other weapons.

This kind of expertise is being spread with great enthusiasm—something apparent from the helmets, dogs, gas masks used by demonstrators at the Pentagon. The *National Guardian* for November 4, 1967, goes into great detail about the purchase of proper equipment. The helmet recommended is a fiberglass one from Japan. Leather jackets, boots, blue jeans, gloves, give padding against clubs. Picket signs should be chosen for their usefulness as body shields, sign poles for their stoutness in warding off blows. Rope, flashlights, pen knives, maps and aerial photos are recommended to the compleat demonstrator.

At the *National Guardian's* annual dinner in New York last year, Rap Brown called for the Left to aid the black rebellion: "If you can't see yourself in the context of being John Brown, then bring me the guns. . . . If you can't give a gun, then give a dollar to somebody who can buy a gun." It is a rhetoric that goes with the fall mood of students in 1967, when campus insurgency became openly militant. It was the old pattern, student unrest following (after a slight lag) the development of the "civil rights" movement. Much of this chest-pounding looks juvenile—though the same was said of Berkeley, which began the escalation of campus rebellion; it is hard to take it seriously. But those who grow up breathing talk of war in the streets —who live every day with the threat of arrest, or of injury; who move about regularly "under the gun"—develop a tolerance of violence, even as the weapons of violence accumulate everywhere. Henry Ward Beecher, who called in the eighteen-fifties for guns around the Bible, grew up during the thirties in a town and on a campus (Oberlin) where riots took place on the issues of free speech and slavery. One day his sister Hattie (who, as Mrs. Stowe, would write *Uncle Tom's Cabin*) came in and found him pouring hot lead into molds. "What on earth are you doing, Henry?" He answered, "Making bullets to kill men with." They were small lead seeds of the large crates, later delivered, full of Beecher's Bibles. Idealism and violence can feed each other in the young.

The thing that links student and Negro restiveness is opposition to "the Establishment," opposition growing, of course, out of deep belief in it, in its power and conspiratorial purpose. Over against "them," one has a clear sense of "us." The Establishment explains one's own feeling of victimization. Moving from group to group in the Pentagon march, I heard people describe with undisguised enjoyment the massive retaliation into which our government had been prodded—the meshing of military gears against the marchers; sifting of government spies through their number; the attendant clank of Power all around them, hedging them in. All this was a fleshing of the students' inner vision, which explains the satisfaction so many got from a day that looks futile or inconclusive to outsiders. It was a confirmation, to participants, of all the improbable things these kids had been saying—that the government was bent on repression, was afraid of them; was an Emperor without clothes, who must quiet all children's voices; a military machine gone mad, powerful but insecure; on the edge, always, of electronic panic.

Yet the armored realization of their insight did not satisfy most marchers. They had to add imagined terrors to the palpable military presence. I did not see all parts of the march, of course; I cannot say that brutalities did not take place in other sectors. But I know how rumor magnified the things I *did* see; how, out at the rim of the crowd, vicarious wounds became more spectacular than the actual ones I saw inflicted in the front lines. Even at the Lincoln Memorial, before the crowd passed over the bridge into the mercy of the soldiery, the crowd was masticating its indignities with delectation. A pretty unpainted girl with absentminded hair and eyes, one of "the Diggers" from New York, told me an FBI plot had made some of the marchers' buses cancel out. "The bus companies claimed that drivers would not come down with us, since we were not sure when we were going back; and they were afraid their buses might get damaged. But that was just an excuse. The FBI was behind it, making them cancel." How do you know that? "Because that's the kind of thing they do whenever anyone tries to disagree with them."

That was all her evidence. It was useless to urge that drivers might understandably have qualms about young fares liable to be in jail when their time came to return—that, in short, the stated reason had a certain plausibility. As useless to argue that the FBI would not content itself with canceling several buses (most of whose fares were fitted into cars or trains) if it meant to disrupt travel to Washington, or block access to the city; and that the small gain (if it were one) to be wrested from this maneuver could not possibly balance the risk of setback—of being exposed in the midst of such trivial goings on; that, in short, the conspiratorial explanation was implausible. Ordinary rules of likelihood do not impress the connoisseurs of conspiracy: it is the task of conspirators to make their participation seem implausible.

I found the same distrust of "them" in estimating the number of marchers who reached Washington and crossed the Potomac. The Mobilization Committee, nominally in charge of the protest, had promised to produce 100,000 marchers. District of Columbia police estimated the crowd at 45,000 to 50,000. The Department of Defense released a figure of 30,000 to 35,000; and it did more—it gave to the press those aerial photos, taken at the march's climax, on which it based its count, using techniques developed by foresters (who subdivide the picture by gradations of density). Once again, the risk of doctoring these photos, or miscounting from them, while releasing them for verification at independent photo labs, would be suicidal—and certainly not worth any gain that could be made by belittling the numbers. Yet veterans of the march are still convinced that the government numbers must be false simply because "they" released them. Demonology has its own cogencies.

The sense of victimization, among student marchers as among ghetto residents, is charged with a sexual atmosphere of the subconscious, from which its symbols bubble up. One young professor, writing in *The Atlantic Monthly*, is convinced (on the word of other marchers) that federal marshals "sometimes hit the girls in the breasts instead of the head"; and he paints a Gustave Doré scene of the instant when he saw "an official of the U.S. Department of Justice, presumably acting under orders from the Attorney General's office, club someone to the ground, club, club, and club, and then, when she stops yelling"—the "someone" has been transformed, under the exigencies of that orgasmic "club, club, and club," into a *she*—"drag her off by her hair with an expression on his face like he's just been laid." Gustave Doré? More, perhaps, in the style of "caveman" cartoons.

It is interesting that many of these same marshals were heroes of the left, and demons to the right, when they protected students and marchers during civil rights duty in the South. At that time the deep fears of the *South* were stirred: sexual fantasies, of marshals being favored by black women at night, passed from fevered cracker head to cracker head. Late on the night of the Pentagon march, in the building's cafeteria, I talked with a man who had been in Montgomery, heard him compare that assigment with his present one. I saw many expressions on these marshals' faces, out on the lawn, at the embattled press door, at the top of the crowded main stairs, and inside the cafeteria; I saw fear, disgust, fatigue, contempt. But no marshal I saw had the time, even if he had the inclination, to stop and savor a particular clubbing, or wander dreamily about with a girl in tow, smiling inanely like one "just laid." That vision is granted, I presume, only to those who have undergone the proper spiritual preparation.

The marshals' leisurely orgies of the baton resemble the story I read, in Vaughn's bookshop, of populous sadistic rites in progress at precinct stations during the peak of the Detroit riot. Or the stories that, in the Algiers Motel, the dead men were killed by blasting off their genitals. Or the story that touched off a Harlem riot during the Second World War—here is James Baldwin's description of that story: "Rumor, flowing immediately to the streets outside, stated that the [black] soldier had been shot in the back [by a white policeman], an instantaneous and revealing invention, and that the soldier had died protecting a Negro woman. The facts were somewhat different—for example, the soldier had not been shot in the back, and was not dead, and the girl seems to have been as dubious a symbol of womanhood as her white counterpart in Georgia usually is, but no one was interested in the facts." Exactly. The story had a "symbolic truth" expressing the fear and resentment of the ghetto, not registering facts about some incident that put the match to these resentments. In the Watts riot, rumor went everywhere, and was accepted, that the first women arrested—Mrs. Frye and Joyce Ann Gaines—where both pregnant (neither were); and that the first had been kicked in the stomach, the second had been strangled.

Unfortunately, those who live regularly in this world of "symbolic truth" may find it impossible to accept the standards of a more prosaic truth; they offer their private vision as the objective record of events. The leering caveman in the brain becomes a federal marshal on the Pentagon lawn. What is "truly" expressed is the victim's awareness of himself as a victim. And that awareness, turned back on itself, leads to paranoia.

It is easy to see why the Negro considers himself a victim (because he *is*), and thinks the Establishment is a conspiracy meant to keep him a victim (it *is* determined to do so, largely at unconscious levels). It is less easy to see why middle-class students at the better universities should feel so victimized. Admittedly the students are "superfluous" at this moment of their lives—unwelcome on the job market; not in the family as a child, not forming their own family unit as parents; promised much in the future, but given no present responsibility in our system; dwelling in a no-man's-land well symbolized by the transient life of campus dormitories, which are half barracks, half nursery; asked to fight a war that is increasingly dubious in cause and outcome. But all these grievances become trivial when weighed against the Negro's lot—which may explain why Negro rebels seem less self-pitying than young affluent whites on the picket line. (Listening to the latter, you would think the Pentagon march was the greatest slaughter of innocents since Herod's time.)

Despite these differences, there are also similarities in these two major (and many minor) protests against the established order. For one thing, it is not simply a matter of affluent whites and poor Negroes. A UCLA study of the Watts rioters showed that activists in the black community are not those at the very bottom of the economic ladder, but those who have moved some short way up:

> Our data contradict the common notion that those persons who are the most deprived will sense the greatest frustrations and express the highest levels of discontent. Instead, they support the other contention that those most aggrieved are those who have begun to overcome traditional barriers but who are impatient with the yet existing constraints placed upon them. . . . It appears from our data that this resentment is just as, or more, likely to find expression in riot participation by those who are better off than by those who are disadvantaged.

Revolution is the result of baffled hopes, not of sheer hopelessness. That is why Negro discontent is more aggressively expressed after the advances of the last decade—after the Brown decision and the civil rights laws—than it was during the hopeless earlier years of this century. At last they were given some hope, and given little else. It is at this point that black ghetto hands join with white hands on the campus. No group has had greater hopes raised than the white generation now in college. Their parents moved up the social ladder in the world's most powerful nation. A period of liberal promise said that all problems would be solved by reason. One's children would go even higher, solve more problems, gain more. Reality, for today's students, is tested constantly against this gauzy dream. For this dream persists: the very myth of "the Establishment" is, in radical minds, essentially liberal. The liberal view that history is at the disposal of man's reason leads, inexorably, to the conclusion that evil, if it occurs, is planned; that human frailty and muddle is not to blame for cloudy wars and for rats in the ghetto, for buses that fail to arrive on time and crowds that fail to reach the wished-for mark. The girl whose friends were inconvenienced on their trip to Washington had been brought up expecting buses—and rockets—to run on time for her all her life. Only against the giant measure of this dream can today's student count himself deprived and a victim. And so he rebels against everything except the dream (for the dream is that which *fuels* rebellion).

The cult of revolution goes forward under this tattered banner of innocent hopes unrealized—hopes blocked by the malice of our rulers. The true revolutionary must believe that a system which hinders him is not merely accidental. It is organized. Belief in the *deliberated* malice of the ruler is what steels a rebel to audacities. And this belief now spins a demonology around poor Lyndon Johnson—*personalizing* evil yet making the person larger (and less) than life, a personal *devil*. A recent commercial venture turns out dart games with his face as target. *MacBird*, the sick joke, becomes Garrison's investigation, the sick reality of charges that one President killed another. The souring of a silly dream turns to silly vendetta against one Texan. And this rebellious mood, of conspiracy-weaving and demonology, spreads out from ghetto and campus to taint the whole national atmosphere.

One comforting thing about open profession of revolution on the Left is the theoretical difficulty of forming a revolutionary mystique on the Right. Some rightists—like the Breakthrough group in Detroit—might prepare themselves for what they consider the breakdown of law and order. But it seems impossible for those who *support* law and order to be, simultaneously, professed rebels—or so I thought until I reached Los Angeles.

There I was told about a young right-wing organizer, Ed Butler, whose forthcoming book is called *Revolution Is My Profession.* I met his assistant, Alan Bock, who drove me to Mr. Butler's home in Beverly Hills, where he was entertaining friends. On the trip there, Bock talked above a rattle of soft drinks in the back of his car—odd tumbril sounds for a revolution. Mr. Bock explained to me that Ed had come West from New Orleans about a year ago, to be closer to his patron—Patrick Frawley, the Croesus of the clean-cut adolescent right, whose minstrels sing "Up with People" over the TV. Frawley's vast wealth is drawn from his control of companies like Schick, Eversharp, and Technicolor; it is dispensed on projects meant to stamp out what Mr. Frawley considers the two main evils of the modern world—Communism and alcoholism. That, I was to learn, explained the ominous rattle of Cokes in the back seat. "Ed is starting a magazine, the *Westwood Village Square;* I am assisting him. The *Square* will be a counter to leftist student magazines [literary equivalent of Frawley's strolling minstrels]. Ed has all kinds of irons in the fire, but primarily he considers himself an expert on what he calls 'conflict management.' "

We pulled into a patio-parkinglot, and went in the front door. Mr. Butler rose from a group in his large front room, and foamed toward us, down gray stairs into the hallway, with a sudsy circumfluent greeting. We went up nice gradations of the stairs deeper into gray upholstery and carpet —to a cocktail-less cocktail party. The other guests were an actor and actress, and four or five young representatives of right-wing organizations. Mr. Frawley had been invited, and these bright-eyed unalcoholic folk were ready to interest him, over innocuous bubbles, in their organizational aims (and deficits). A college student who had just been sent by The World Youth Crusade for Freedom to make a lightning tour of Vietnam was describing, when I entered, how he would devastate campus debaters by drawing on this experience. He is warming up for Frawley, who never arrives; all that carbonation went tickling down for naught. The boy left, late in the evening, trying to get Butler to arrange a meeting the next day—before the debater must return to school.

When Vietnam had been bloodily toured, and the actors had given us their screen gossip, I asked Mr. Butler for his theory of conflict management. He is a native of New Orleans, with the lazy economy of Southern speech, which scales as many sounds as possible down to the single vowel *ah* ("*Ah'm* cha*h*med to ca*h*m to tha*h*t subj*ah*ct"). He has wavy blond hair over a handsome face (he could sing with the minstrels any day), and a composed, almost syrupy manner through which sudden gestures and noises erupt— brief thunderclap of laughter, a palm slapped, fingers snapped like firecrackers. He sips, continually, on his favorite soft drink, Mountain Dew, whose praises he had sung as he pressed one on me when I entered.

"This is the century of revolution," he began portentously, "and only a revolutionary can cope with it. The government cannot; it cannot use the propaganda tools of Communist revolutionaries without gaining a tyrannical control over the media. We need private masters of agitprop—professional conflict managers."

I asked how these managers would break up riots in America. "Well, that depends on the circumstances. I have studied this in great detail. You sometimes only need a few people to break up a riot—for instance, by dropping tear grenades in their midst and shouting it is poison gas. Or you can have people mix with the mob, pretending to be part of it but actually clubbing its leaders." ("That's what I'd like to do, get in and hit those sonsabitches," the Vietnam tourist grinned, carried away, perhaps, by too much Mountain Dew.) I said that the tear gas example sounded like a case Rex Applegate had described to me. "Yes, I gave Colonel Applegate some of my ideas, which he incorporated in his book without giving me credit." (I called Applegate later, and found out he had met Butler once, briefly, in Washington.)

I asked whether it would not be an infringement on police power for conflict managers to be breaking up riots. After all, in our form of government the police have a monopoly on violence. "No they don't. The surgeon, for instance, can use a knife on a person. I agree that no one but a professional should be allowed to use violence. But my conflict managers would be professionals." Who will set professional standards? "The managers themselves—as other professionals maintain standards; as the bar gives lawyers the right to practice. But conflict management is more concerned with preventing violence than with using it. Modern wars must be won with this"—he points to his mouth, an instrument of whose magic he is clearly convinced.

How will words stop riots? "The conflict manager will infiltrate troublemaking groups, try to divert them from their goals, break up their structure, create internal dissension." How does this differ from police undercover work? "The police agent gets information and gives it to the authorities for them to act. The professional of conflict management handles his own practice, and is trained to do so." Has this been accomplished anywhere? "Well, all the years I practiced in New Orleans, we never had any trouble. And then, as soon as I leave, you get the Garrison business—a classical case of Communist propaganda." Do you think Garrison a Communist? "No, he's being used." What did you do to prevent such occurrences when you were there? "Well, I exposed Lee Harvey Oswald for what he was; and shortly afterward he left town."

He is referring to the fact that, on a radio talk show with two co-hosts, Oswald was one of three guests, and Butler was another. After this broadcast (one of two radio shows on which Oswald was questioned), Butler billed himself as "the only propaganda specialist ever to confront Oswald in person." He put out a phonograph record—*Oswald: Self-Portrait in Red*—containing the transcript of that radio show and his own commentary on Oswald. Then he made a movie—*Hitler in Havana*—claiming that Oswald was inspired to his act by Castro propaganda. This caught the eye of Mr. Frawley, whose Schick company sponsored TV showings of the film.

The thirty-three-year-old Butler has an extraordinary gift for self-promotion. After a slow start—he drifted in and out of various high schools, dropped out of Loyola College in New Orleans, was drafted into the army—he discovered his true metier when he went through an army Management School at Fort Belvoir. He had entertained some ambitions as an illustrator (he drew the cover portrait of Oswald on his phonograph album), but here he first realized that his artistry must be with words—with slogans, propaganda, promotion. He conceived the idea of setting up a propaganda center in New Orleans, where there are Cuban refugees (and money to be spent on their plight)— an idea that became INCA, the Information Council of the Americas. Using this as a base, Butler developed his ideas on conflict management, got Louisiana Congressman Hale Boggs interested in his work, gave speeches, handed out awards, received awards, was praised by Senator Dirksen and Senator Mundt. He raised funds to train a whole school of professional conflict managers, who would convert America's defense system from a passive to a dynamic one, actively propagandizing around the world: "The military segments of the dynamic defense are primarily an official prerogative, but do not preclude private activity in the guerrilla, sabotage, and insurgency efforts." Most of the early work was aimed at equipping propaganda guerrillas for Latin American countries. But the speech from which this last quote comes was circulated again in 1966, with the notation that its comments on the need for conflict management were made "one year before Watts." He admits that "Communist-style conflict management without a worthwhile goal is anti-democratic"; but thinks he supplies the worthwhile goal—the continuing American Revolution, against which all later rebellions are "counterrevolutionary." He thinks this does not go against ordained law enforcement, because "we the people" are the ultimate ones who have to "provide for the common defense," and the Constitution itself allows citizens to bear arms. Even the right wing, then, is producing its Che Guevaras, scribbling manifestos in their cushy retreats; men like Ed Butler, who is smoother than any Lobsinger, more swinging than Bob Welch, glib as the "Up with People" singers—and convinced that revolutionary tactics are a regular instrument, now, of our domestic politics.

8 "LIKE IT IS"

Men do not like to be protected, it emasculates them.

—James Baldwin

I spent all one day and two long nights with Hutch and Duke. When we were not drinking somewhere, we were driving somewhere—the two of them up front, I a captive audience in back (where both handles were gone from the rear doors). Whenever Hutch's heavy foot stabbed us forward or cuffed us to a stop, weapons rattled in the trunk—clubs, two shotguns, a sawed-off rifle, sawed-off shotgun (these last the gift of solicitous teen-agers worried for their safety). Hutch and Duke both have a "natural." Hutch wears leaded gloves. The two of them give palm-out shoved fist salutes to the "brothers" they see everywhere, and exchange militant greetings—"B.P., baby" (Black Power). They owe their present status—one they relish almost childishly—to the riots; and they know this. They are Deputy Sheriffs of Cook County.

Sheriff Woods, an ex-FBI man—the tough guy who told his men in Maywood they must shoot carefully, no time could be wasted on trips to the hospital—cast about, during the Detroit riot, for someone to be his eyes and ears at the trouble points around Chicago—Markham, Phoenix,

Harvey, Chicago Heights. Two young process servers had written a memorandum to him earlier in the summer, describing sensitive spots and criticizing the way they were being handled. Both had been organizers of a political group (The New Breed) that was out at the edge of militancy in 1964 (the black cause counts in months as others count in decades, it is a movement led by the young). The New Breed never adopted Dr. King's nonviolence (though the group served as marshals for King's Chicago march)—in fact, they were among the first to open a karate school for teaching brothers self-defense. They struck a bargain with Charles Percy—that he finance their local candidate if they support him in his '64 campaign. It was a one-shot affair. "He'll find it does not last in '68," Hutch says. "We tried to tell him not to come into our territory playing poor boy. 'Drive a Cadillac,' I said to him—'Then we'll know you have good sense.' But he wanted to impress the whites with pictures of him in the ghetto wearing shirt sleeves."

Neither of the two make any bones about their grievances with white men in general, and white cops in particular. They are working on a book to be called *Two Bigots*. Nonetheless, Sheriff Woods made them his County Youth Division, sent them into Markham; and, almost immediately, they disarmed a vigilante group of older Negroes and a young gang that had been causing trouble. The gang turned in eleven shotguns and thirteen pistols. The Sheriff's appointment of the two men seemed, I said to Hutch, an enlightened decision: "He's not enlightened. He's something better. He's fair; and he's the most *truthful* law enforcement agent I have ever met. He knows what he does not know." The two bigots, both of them fidgety in police circles, all touchy edges, are proud of their job because they took it on their own terms: "He *has* to let us remain black, because we're no possible use to him except as black men, able to talk with the brothers. If it comes to a war between blacks and whites—well, it's pretty clear where we will be." The two get along with the teen-agers they help because their attitude is that the quickest way to stop police brutality is to *be* the policeman in the neighborhood. They don't like to have things done for them, and they challenge the kids to take the same attitude. "We don't tell them to be model citizens. We tell them not to be stupid. Stick together; use the gangs they have; form co-ops; get into business; *own* something. These kids react to money."

Hutch—James R. Hutchinson—is tall, good-looking in a baby-faced way, deceptively youthful and willowy in appearance, but a trained strong athlete—high-school and college basketball, "airborne" in Vietnam, karate teaching at the school. He likes to flick his leaded gloves, with their built-in sap, within inches of one's face, to demonstrate control. He is the scholar of the pair, in a constant boil of statistics, running over with percents and averages—"85 percent" recurring with suspicious frequency (it seems his only way of saying "a large number").

Duke—Leonard Hunter—is a little shorter than Hutch, and one year older (twenty-seven). He dresses with panache—his wasp-waist wrapped around with colorful vests, his suits pinched in, cut close and tight. He speaks in a husky precise voice, picking out key syllables for emphasis. "Man, that is *eh*-vident." He moves in a constant pummeling seizure of hoarse laughter, benevolent "dry heaves" brought on by the craziness of things. The world has him at its mercy; it overpowers him with idiocy. After describing how the University of Chicago claimed it would improve the lot of Negroes by clearing them out of its vicinity, he doubles over as if punched and wheezes out: "Them cats sure can sell a story (*uh! uh! uh!*)"

All liberal projects seem to have earned their scorn. Urban renewal—"nigger removal." Public housing—"highrise slums." The Poverty Program—"Our kids all realize they were just being paid to do nothing." Moving Negroes out toward the suburbs—"Get us out of the city before we can control it; the *Damn* [for Dan] Ryan Expressway is our Berlin Wall, we can't cross back except by daylight."

And, once again, Patrick Moynihan is the villain. Hutch
leads the attack, with statistics: "He says sixty percent of
the illegitimate births are Negro children. But he neglects
to mention that ninety percent of the abortions are performed for whites—and the hospitals will cover up the
illegitimate births of white women." Duke is doubled over
again: "What that cat knows about us colored boys I could
put in my eyeball." They reject the whole history of the
white man's attempts to help them: "Roosevelt hurt the hell
out of us," Hutch says. "He started paying us for doing
nothing; that destroyed our self-respect." Duke: "That cat
was a genius! Just think—*uh! uh! uh!*—they say he loved
another woman, but kept his wife too. I bet she said, 'Do
you want a divorce?' and he said, 'No, baby, it would hurt
my image.' "

I asked them what they would put in place of the old
liberal measures. They take different approaches when they
answer. Hutch's analysis is in terms of sex. "The white man
has split our community from within. He hires the Negro
woman; over seventy-six percent of the married Negro
women work." (There goes Duke again: "Man, does that
sound like *unemployment?*") "He doesn't have to pay her
as much as he would pay to a man; and then she thinks—the
white establishment is not so bad, there must be something
wrong with that cat of hers at home, who *doesn't* get hired.
Who does the buying in our community? Who does the
voting?—eighty-five percent of the precinct captains in our
district are women. Daley knows what he is doing. He
appoints Bernardine Washington to his Human Rights
Commission. She knows about as much of what's going on
in the street as A. Philip Randolph does. He puts Mrs.
Wendell Green on the school board. Negro boys have no
male image to look up to. Patricia Harris gets the job of
Ambassador to Luxembourg, though her husband has the
same degree she has. In proportion, we have more female
judges than you do. Now, men are ninety percent ego—so
black men can't stand the contempt their women have for

them. That is why ninety-five percent of the interracial marriages are of Negro men and white women—women who have been brought up in a tradition of respect for the male." I mentioned that white women also own more property than men now. Duke is sneezing helplessly over this one: "Y'all cats die quicker, leaving all that bread behind. We might just play a waiting game, and get your women *and* your money." Hutch agrees that male superiority is an idea being undermined in the white community. "But you control the media; so when this gets too bad, you just put out a lot of movies about the sad lady tycoon who returns to the home and is happy taking care of sixteen kids.

"The Negro boy gets second-best at home," Hutch drives ahead, his steam up now. "The girl is the one who will get jobs, stay in school, be given consideration by the white community. Why, eighty-five percent of Negro women say they would send a girl to school before they would send their boy. The Negro boy is not only rebelling against the white man, but against Momma. That's why ninety-five percent of the rioters are boys." (In Watts, when young Marquette Frye was arrested for speeding, he joked with officers until his mother arrived on the scene and accused him of being drunk; only then did he turn surly—and the riot began.)

"Not only is the boy rebelling against Momma; he's rebelling against his Mommized elders. You know, the average age on the South Side is twenty-five; on the West Side, it's nineteen. There is a big communications gap between the kids and the adults, and an even bigger gap between the adults and the white man. So when the white man tries to deal with the kids he has two gaps he must bridge. *One* would be hard enough. But you know what he does? He chooses exactly the wrong people to deal with—the women, the 'older leaders,' the womanized men!"

Duke's approach is more economic than sexual: "There are too many hands in our pockets. We'd get along just fine if you only let us handle the vice in our area. But we don't even run our own numbers. The syndicate, the big markets, the slumlords—they take twenty-eight billion a year just off the cash register. Money comes into the ghetto at nine in the morning; and all of it leaves again by five at night. One of the white boys we worked with in the campaign said 'You all are pretty hot numbers when it comes to sex.' I said 'You think so? Let's make a deal. We'll trade you, for all y'all cats' money' (*uh! uh!*)."

Hutch agrees: "One of our thirteen-year-old kids put it as well as anyone could: 'There's nothing the matter with niggers that money can't solve.' But every time you see a house torn down in the ghetto, you can bet that a supermarket or a gas station is going up to get that money just as soon as it is in our pockets. They don't want us to own anything, any of the businesses, to keep something of what we earn. The money is not so important in itself—it is the pride that comes from owning, from having economic independence."

Duke is not doubling up anymore; he rivals the Fat Boy in *Pickwick* for his ability to catnap anywhere, any time, when the action gets slow. He has heard Hutch's pitch before. I haven't—we talk past two in the morning; he is eager, now, to serve up concrete proofs. Nothing will do but a drive, that morning, to the major "El" stops where workers leave for the day's employment. "But we'll have to hit them before six A.M."

So, after less than two hours of sleep, I tottered out onto Michigan Avenue; the wind off the Lake sliced me in little pieces, which blew here and there till Hutch collected them and dumped me in the back seat of his sheriff's car (the one without handles in the back, a convenience for transporting prisoners). Hutch looks disgustingly fresh, but Duke is flaked out again—he went on to more action, refreshed after his nap (and our talk) ended last night. Another deputy is with them, William Smith. Smitty, an experienced policeman in his forties, agrees with Hutch and Duke about the problems of the Negro boy. He went to see the mother of one twelve-year-old who was always in trouble; all she did was insult the boy in front of Smitty. Later Smitty had the boy adopted, and there has been no trouble since. We drive past high-rise slums. "That's where you keep *down* with the Joneses," Smitty says. "Can you imagine coming home at night to a football stadium of noise?" Duke is paroxysms: "The politicians did a *good* job there."

Our first stop is 63rd and Cottage Grove. Buses humph their doors open and shut; women pour out of them and up the El stairs—well dressed, the younger ones miniskirted ("Any higher," Smitty whews, "we'd have to run her in for indecent exposure"); the older ones in furs; those in between wear leather or plastic coats, pink or white. "They're going to scrub floors," Hutch says; "but they go in furs." "Well," Duke explains, "some of them are going to those big homes out in the suburbs. Man, our people travel in some pretty high circles" (the soft dry detonations punctuate his words). Hutch is all business: "How many natural hairdos do you see on the women?" The hair is red, blue, indescribable tints; piled high, pulled low; wound in taffy configurations. "They're pretending they are white. The woman buys white style for herself and her daughter. The boys have to shift for themselves. If a Negro man gets a smile out of a woman during the day, it's a real accomplishment." Smitty laughs: "He's really going some to catch *her* attention. Man, he's got to be de*licious*." "That's why the cats go out and buy the best when they get money—forty-dollar shoes, fifty-dollar knits" [sweaters]. "Man, they take off their knits before they let themselves get into a fight," Duke manages to get out with his customary effort. "We told Chuck Percy, 'Whatever you do, don't fool with a cat's knits!' But he went up to a guy and stuck one of his campaign buttons right into it; and this cat pushed him away in utter amazement—" 'What are you *doing* to my knit?' "

A few men climb the El stairs; they all seem to carry attaché cases. "Janitors," Smitty guesses. "Yeah, they carry coveralls in the cases; that's how bad they need some dignity," Hutch says in his emotional voice. He does not laugh at the world's turns, as Duke can. A man drives his wife up, drops her off at the stairs: "Now he'll go home —no job. And the car is hers, no doubt." A young man goes by wearing a natural. "Hi-brothers!" with the fist-push. "Hey-brother." "You notice," Hutch twists around to me, "it's 'Hi-brother.' You don't use the word 'sister' much in greeting the girls. It's 'Hi-baby' to them. The *brotherhood* is what our young boys need. The gangs used to be the only masculine world they knew. Now the whole teen-age crowd is one gang of brothers."

To illustrate his point, he drives me, after we hit a few more El stops, to "The Wall of Respect" at 43rd and Langley—a stretch of "blind side" brick wall on which a black pantheon was painted last summer. Elijah Muhammad, Muhammad Ali, Rap Brown, Lew Alcindor, Jimmy Brown, Ray Charles. It is a male world, painted with uneven skills, at different scales, crude yet somehow attaining majesty. It stretches along the sides of four buildings. "That signifies unity," Smitty says; and he points out that there are no blemishes on the wall. Every other brick surface in sight is scribbled over, pocked, smeared. But this one is unmarked, fresh as the day it was painted. There are children on the corner, waiting for a bus. "What does that mean to you?" Smitty asks, pointing to the wall. "I don't know. It's just beautiful," they say, wide-eyed—apprentice young knights in the new chivalry. "Would you ever mark it up?" "NO." Why not? "That would be *wrong*." It is said that Negroes, put in bright new housing, just deface and ruin it. Not if all their walls were Walls of Respect. "Respect, you notice," Hutch nudged me. "Dignity!"

We drive through streets still dingy with night; a lemony sky makes the litter glow first as day gets down to the streets. Women are out, walking to their buses. "They are not afraid to be on the streets. Who rapes men?—and they are the men of the community." "We'll take you to Spiegel's mail order house," Duke suggests, "to see what the work force is." Inside the vast store, we visit an employment area, where classes of new workers shuttle through continually. We see two groups of twenty or so, and not one man in either. Hutch asks the girls what they will be earning their first few months there. Duke has better luck, though, coaxing answers out with winks.

As we drive, Hutch remembers his days in Vietnam: "I went airborne, counterinsurgency; trying to prove something, I guess. I don't know why I fucked around in those jungles all those months. But I do know the brothers who are coming back won't let themselves be pushed around anymore." When we get back into the car after a stop, Hutch checks in on the car radio, "10-8" (back in circulation), then continues with the kind of chatter he heard from planes in Vietnam: " 'Straight Arrow? This is Lone Ranger, about four hundred miles off'—they'll rendezvous in about twelve seconds. 'Oh-uh-vah and ahw-oh-oot,' " he drawls in expert mimicry. "Oh them crackers!"

Hutch and Duke are with the county sheriff's office; but they introduce me to several members of the Chicago city department—Human Relations Division. These men, like Smitty, are Negro cops who came up the hard way, who are called on now to help decipher the ghetto. One, a huge fellow with easy smiling ways, said: "You could always tell a black cop, even in plainclothes—by his size. He was hired to beat up on his own people, and he had to be big. They didn't much care what else he did. One officer—I'll call him Ted—was a known pickpocket; but no one quarreled with him when he was on a case, so the force just ignored his foible. Once a man did make the mistake of taking him on. Ted was waiting for the bus, at his neighborhood stop, and a man started pestering a woman. Ted told him to stop it, and the man whipped out a switchblade. But before he could get it up, his wrist was slashed with Ted's blade. 'Why, Ted,' the lady said, 'I thought you were a policeman.' 'Oh, I forgot,' he mumbled; put his blade away, and pulled his gun."

"Once a cop, a man was not out of the ghetto. Or if he did make the move, it was a slow process. I remember my first cases in the white community. This little lady had called the police, on a burglary, so I went. She nearly fainted when she opened the door and saw me. I told her, 'This won't come off if I come in; but, on the other hand, I never investigate a case on the porch with the screen latched.' Once I got in and she found herself unraped, it went all right." This man, for all his easygoing way, had the fire in his belly. Once another officer "let that word slip"—"I slapped him once across the face, nearly took his jaw off. But I don't believe in violence. Oh, once in a while, you have to be a little mean, especially at home—you know, open the door on the _hinge_ side, for a change? Still, my motto is, Never send a guy away mad. If you mess with me, I may have to pull your dick off. But I won't send you away mad." He describes the way he disciplines his children, whom he is sending to a Catholic school—"Yeah, giving some more money to Louisiana Fats." Louisiana Fats? "Sure, Cardinal Cody."

He is a type of the Negro cop who is suddenly _asked_ to say things about the Negro's feelings that would have got him fired ten years ago. "They want to know who's bitter. We're _all_ bitter. Big surprise!" I talked to a man in Baltimore who came back from service in World War Two, and needed a job. He tried for two years to take the police test, and succeeded, at last, only because his fiancée had a job with the city and got her boss to help (how Hutch would love the story, another proof for his book: the woman could get the job—and even get her man a job—but only by being there first). The man is now a Community Re-

lations officer: "They tell me to go out and find what
'their' complaints are. Hell, I know what the complaints
are. I'm one of 'them.' My complaints are that over a
third of the Baltimore police don't even live in Baltimore.
They lifted the residence requirement in the fifties, to
keep the force from going Negro." In Watts, a Negro
policeman was sent incognito into the riot area to scout the
situation. As he came out to report, he hailed a radio car,
which stopped. The officer inside leaned out and said:
"What you want, shitass jigaboo?" What does a Negro
cop say when his superiors ask what "their" grievances
are? A Negro plainclothesman was beaten by white officers
in the Newark riot.

Hutch told me the brothers were drifting, that night
in Chicago, to one of two meetings—a benefit for a local
leader, and a dinner-talk meant to raise money for Father
Groppi, leader of the Milwaukee open-housing marches.
Reverend Cleage had told me, in Detroit, that open housing is no longer a real issue—"We don't think it's all that
great a thing to live next door to a white man"—and that
marches were a thing of the past: "Oh, there might come
a time when mass presence would have some effect; but it
will be a different kind of thing. It won't be just marching
up the street to say something. This time we'll be going
somewhere, like to tie up town for twenty-four hours
—if we figure it is worth five thousand black people getting
whipped to show a city can't move without us. But just
the old peaceful nonviolent marching, where the white
people throw bricks and stones and you just redeem 'em
through love, that's all *gone*."

I wondered, then, what he thought of Father Groppi,
still marching, still asking for an occupancy law. He smiled
almost beatifically: "*Beautiful*, baby, it's so *nostalgic*. The
last of the marches. Don't you understand?—black people
are looking for confrontations. Anything you want to set
up, they'll make it an issue if you don't consult them. If

you say this street is going to be one way, and don't ask us what *we* want, we'll make it an issue from now till doomsday, and we don't even care about the street. Those marching with Groppi don't care about open occupancy. But still it's a good fight."

I asked Hutch what he thought of Father Groppi. "Oh, he's out of it. He's still marching. We're past the marching stage." But he knew some of the brothers throwing the dinner, so he got us in. After the meal I went up to the stormy priest, incongruously short and quizzical; a sacerdotal Woody Allen, limp weedy locks on a receding hairline, sad-dog eyes, squash nose. Can you win your fight for open occupancy? "There are signs of it." A "Commando" —one of his teen-age entourage—comes up and claps "Grop" on the shoulder. "I see you've let the hair cover your scar," Grop says, brillo-ing a head wound out of the "natural." "Keep that visible. I'm proud of it." "So am I," the Commando beams. "A policeman gave it to him," Groppi tells me. Hutch points out, in a whisper, that the only girl with the party of Commandos is a white one.

The talk is given in a large high-school auditorium. Father Groppi sits flanked by his eight Commandos—bodyguards are the style in this aggressively masculine movement. The Fruit of Islam guarding Elijah Muhammad. The Deacons guarding Southern marchers. The Panthers in California. The devout Zulu trailing Reverend Cleage. The priest's style at the lectern is also Woody Allen, hems and haws and hair-mussing, but exquisitely timed. "*I* don't know, but . . ." he begins when he knows very well. He tells how his angry Commandos tore up the Milwaukee mayor's office: "The white people said 'How shocking!' The Mayor said 'Hoodlums!' And we just said"—his voice sinks to a chortled sexy croon—"Black Power, brother, Black Power."

Though the performance is getting to him, Hutch still tries to pooh-pooh Groppi, and buzzes with sociology:

"You will notice that there are very few women here; and most of the women are white" (and most of the white women are nuns). But now Groppi nets Hutch in with the rest of the rapt audience. "I bet there isn't a black woman in my parish, a white man hasn't tried to make out with her." He tells of a black picnic some whites tried to break up: "Fifteen or twenty Commandos came streaming out of the bus and WHOOSH the whites just disappeared." Clutch in, throat shifting down, to chortle: "It was a beautiful sight. And all the Youth Council cheered—especially, I might say, the young ladies." "Hey," Hutch says with a start, "he does understand." At the press conference after his talk, Father Groppi agrees that his is the last march—the weary appeals cannot go on forever. What next? "Perhaps guerrilla warfare."

Father Groppi seems to experience, in his priesthood, a challenged masculinity that tunes him in on the young Negro's struggle. He describes with glee the Commandos' muscle; uses obscenity with an adolescent's pride in the achievement; describes a school principal who ran, hands flapping in fairy helplessness, through his corridors sobbing "The Commandos are here! The Commandos are here!" (The nuns loved this one.) Asked about his duty to superiors, he has said, "The white priest that has to ask the archbishop every time he crosses the street should never have been ordained—he's a pansy." He has reached his audience now; he is "telling it like it is."

Telling it like it is—not so much a matter of *what* one says, though it is often framed that way. "We trust Stokely Carmichael," Hutch says, "because he never lied to us." Asked about several Negro leaders in Chicago, he answers, "They bullshitted us." They did not, so much, lie; far worse, they *lost touch*. They adopted the white man's language, in which the brothers feel ill-defended. It is so easy to make a slip, be tricked, be laughed at. The whole tongue and idiom are an instrument that belongs to whites, and it would be foolish to challenge them on their own ground. That is why there has been a retreat to the old scorned "Rastus, suh" and "sugah-chile" dialect—soul talk. It is home ground, where the white man cannot follow; or, if he does, where *he* is the one who misses tone and nuance, talks as an outsider. This is where the black man can be at ease, able to laugh at the white man—and at himself. It is where the Lenny-Bruce edge on those speeches at Cambridge gets softened into Duke's sense of irony. "Telling it like it is" is being attuned to the brothers' needs; and the evidence of attunement is up-to-date fluidity of language. Hutch, talking to me one moment about "the sociology of matriarchy," pitches his voice higher and rasps "Hi y'all, you uptight?" when he sees a brother approach. He is bilingual now. If he ever loses touch with those sounds of the street, he will be a lost brother, no longer "telling it like it is."

A white newsman talking to black men is urged, over and over, to tell it like it is. But that is impossible. Perhaps, for a while, a Father Groppi can speak out of analogous resentments and hit the right tone. Some can venture pastiche; use words carefully weighed, loved, worried, eased into place. But it is false, part of the smothering falsehood Hutch and Duke resent in the liberal. They admire Sheriff Woods because he knows he does not know. Their scorn is reserved for people pretending they understand, who don't. People saying they can solve the Negro's problem, who can't. People thinking they have earned a share in Negro pain, who haven't. Those who mother the black men who are trying to grow up. The helpful, the well-meaning. The Moynihans.

I asked Hutch repeatedly why he, with his analysis of Negro matriarchy, resents Moynihan, whose report—whatever its defects—makes the same point Hutch labors at with all his figures and percentages. "Do you think black men would tell the truth to Moynihan?" was all he could answer. He is evasive, unsure of his reasons, sure only of his response. Moynihan did not tell it like it is—he couldn't; he is white.

The Negro does not want to be diagnosed; he does not even want to be helped, if the white man is going to do the helping. He has to do it himself. He wants not help but reparation, not charity but justice. He would rather demand than have things volunteered to him. As Dr. Cleage put it, he is looking for confrontations—and he will find them.

At almost every police department I visited, I asked the superintendent or commissioner one question: How do we prevent riots? In almost every case, I was told: "First, you remove the *causes* of rioting, and our wonderful Mayor is doing this." Then, after this *pro forma* opening, they got down to brass tacks: flood the streets with blue; have good plans, good intelligence; more men, more guns, cars, tear gas, tanks. They know the causes cannot be removed by next summer, or the summer after. Hutch knows it, too: "Give Stokely Carmichael all the power he asks for, and it would still be twenty years before he could accomplish what he wants." Nonetheless, the cry is "Freedom *now.*"

Freedom. Not Utopia. The slums will not disappear *now*. But respect can be built faster than cities. When police commissioners described how their mayor was "removing causes," they talked of eliminating poverty. But money is not the solution in itself. More important is the way the money is gained by the Negro. It must not be given, but surrendered, on his terms, or he will think it is another bribe to "keep him in his place"—paying him for doing nothing. As Malcolm X put it: "A man who tosses worms in the river isn't necessarily a friend of the fish." Given all the money he needs, the Negro would still "seek confrontations" if he were not respected. In spirit he must come for the money, and carry it away, in that dignified attaché case.

The lessons Hutch taught me so graphically at El stops and hiring offices, through the long day in the car and the long night at the Groppi rally, is a lesson that has been spelled out many times, and should have been learned by us long before Moynihan put it in his famous report. The late Richard Wright put the whole Negro horror in a brief story, "Man of All Work," about a Negro who cannot get a job until he dresses up in women's clothes. That experience—of being spiritually hidden, covered, smothered in women's clothes—shrieks at us, in many ways, from Baldwin's work, as when one of his characters says: "Then, one fine day, the guy feels chilly between his legs and feels around for his cock and balls and finds she's helped herself to them and locked them in the linen closet."

Hutch raging at all the women precinct captains in Chicago is like Claude Brown, describing Adam Powell's rise to power in Harlem: "The women, with their votes, just ran the community. They'd elect the councilmen. They'd elect our same old light, bright, damn-near-white Congressman. . . . As Johnny D. once said, a woman's brain is between her legs, and some pretty nigger who was suave, like our good Congressman, could get up there and say, 'Look, baby, I'm going to do this and that for you.' The women would go right out and vote for him, because the nigger was too pretty for them not to. We kept on getting the same treatment because the women were running Harlem."

A patronizing attitude castrates—which is the reason some militants say they prefer open white hatred to the liberal's condescension. And they find that one way to be respected, to be *noticed* at least, is to be feared. For many, it is a big step up. After all, Hutch and Duke have their jobs because of the white man's fear. Men who looked condescendingly on "colored *boys*" now edge around them. They are Commandos, Deacons, Panthers, bodyguards, knights; they are men. They will be proving that, to us and to themselves, now and next summer and the next. They will be playing with fire, daring the white man, putting whitey (and themselves) to the test. What this means, I suppose, is that, like little boys in a strange new playground, we must fight before we can be friends.

Any one of these confrontations can ignite another Detroit, or worse. It is unrealistic to expect a society to overlook this possibility; or—having recognized it—not to take precautions. If the police have a simplistic view of "removing the causes," black leaders take a silly view of the "guns or butter" issue as it applies to civil disturbance. They say that if the money spent on riot weapons were given to them, there would be no danger of a riot. "Chicago spent three million dollars extra last summer," Hutch claims, "just on riot patrol—the manhours, the cars, the fuel, the maintenance. If that went to us, they wouldn't need patrols." But he himself says that money cannot do it—not unless there is a creative friction that makes men bristle with new respect. And this friction has no chance of becoming creative unless it is in some measure controlled. The Cambridge black nationalists admit that when they want the bigger guns—state troopers and National Guard—called in rather than the smaller, wilder fire of local cops.

The danger is that white society cannot bear with patience the attritive ordeal of these confrontations—that private citizens will take arms; or that they will demand, of elected officials or of the police, that the confrontations be brought to an end. This possibility is a grim one. Just how grim, Richard Rovere told us last autumn: "I can imagine the coming to power of an American de Gaulle, or even of someone a lot more authoritarian than de Gaulle. Much of the troublemaking in the months and years ahead will be the work of Negroes, and I can even imagine the imposition of a kind of American apartheid—at least in the North, where Negroes live in ghettos that are easily sealed off. If there should be the will to do it, it could be done quite 'legally' and 'Constitutionally.' There are enough smart lawyers around to figure out how." Other voices grow increasingly pessimistic. The war budgets and plans and armaments are there; and the revolutionary restlessness is bound, in David-moments, to tempt Goliath.

But a man like Dr. Cleage wants to be mayor of Detroit —so he wants a Detroit to be mayor of. Who would rule a cinder? The threat of police blitzkrieg on the one side, of guerrilla terrorism on the other, are reaching that "unthinkable" stage which made atomic weapons, in Churchill's estimate, maintain world peace throughout the fifties. What Adam Powell calls "the Second Civil War" is not a possibility, but present reality—anyone who denies that is *certainly* not telling it like it is. But it is a Cold War, a test of nerves, a series of feints—and it must increasingly be confined to that. The confrontations must be symbolic; the opponent must be allowed to save face—to retire with his briefcase. It is good to know about, and fear, the guns we all live under. Otherwise, God help us, we may use them.

Knowledge that the guns are there gives new urgency to the task of preventing white vigilantism. As I stood in the Beverly Hills home and heard the young man say he would like to "bash the sonsabitches," I thought to myself: Starting with Hutch? Starting with Duke?

The presence of the guns makes it imperative to develop limited-response weapons, and train men in their intricacies, so the police will not be panicked into total response— flexible weapons that allow a long "escalation" of riot techniques, putting off and off the need for heavy arms. It means that we cannot hope, by some drastic measure, to make all the danger go away; that we must learn to live with danger, and limit it, and survive, all of us; so that, having fought, we may be friends.

EPILOGUE

It was a dream fall, my body languid and
fastidious as to where to land, until the
floor became impatient and smashed up
to meet me.

—Ralph Ellison

Policemen see ghetto residents as an army; see them in the mass, as menacing. And residents of the ghetto see cops as prison guards commissioned to "keep them in their place," in prison. Seen in the mass, the movement of these armies looks like a slow deadly ballet, like a war. And the attitude of these "combatants" is spreading out. Other parts of the white community feel new solidarity with their armed police—vigilante groups, inner-city whites, naïve defenders of "law and order." Still other groups— like the student rebels—stand over against the police and the hated "Establishment," thus indirectly (and sometimes directly) closing ranks with black militants and rioters. A heightening tension and rhetoric infect us all. Party politics degenerates into demonology. Everyone talks of his particular rebellion—ridiculously, even of "rebellion" against crime: "The time has come when the American people are going to rise up and revolt against the lawbreakers in this country" (thus Robert McNamara, in November of

1967, trying to recruit policemen from the ranks of men returned from Vietnam).

New studies come out every day, painting a black picture. New weapons are developed and bought—police are buying the ceramic armored vests which, in Vietnam, repel armor-piercing bullets; firemen ask for armored vests too, and for bulletproof windows on their trucks. Panels are summoned, to hear distressing news—as when a Columbia sociologist warned the President's Commission on Civil Disorders of "expanding guerrilla warfare between the races until the entire country becomes a tinderbox, like South Africa." The country shifts into new patterns of hostility, and hardens there. Looking at this large pattern, we can see ourselves moving, inevitably, mindlessly, toward internecine war.

But if one moves closer to these "armies," he finds individual faces:

—the scared Negro children of Cambridge, playing football near fire-gutted buildings, admirers of Unitas;

—extraordinary compassionate cops like Ray Girardin and General Gelston;

—Reverend Albert Cleage, who (while Detroit burns) burns to be mayor of Detroit;

—Richard Henry, dreaming of Chinese subs in inescapably American terms, talking of expeditions to Israel and the Eskimos, of technology and nuclear plants, of reparations given when a U.S. mail truck hits a dog (wild visions of beneficent law);

—and Duke;

—and Hutch.

Is it true we can find no room for these people, cannot hold them together in peace? It is hard to imagine how we are to avoid war, if one looks only at the faceless assembling and arming of "hostiles." But look once on the faces of the individuals, and it is hard to imagine our being such idiots as to go to war with ourselves. Albert Cleage says the black man is an intelligence test the white man is taking. The things I have reported in this book confront us with a definite, shaped challenge: they are an intelligence test we all are taking, a final exam.

ABOUT THE AUTHOR

Garry Wills, born in 1934 in Atlanta, Georgia, was trained as a classicist, receiving his Ph.D. from Yale, and taught ancient Greek at the Johns Hopkins University for five years before becoming a free-lance writer and a contributing editor of *Esquire* magazine. He is the author of *Chesterton, Politics and Catholic Freedom, Roman Culture,* and coauthor (with Ovid Demaris) of *Jack Ruby,* which The New American Library published in 1968.